Captain's Log ASA Documente

Dates   Leave: _____   Arrive: _____

Times   Leave: _____   Arrive: _____

Location

Origin: _____

Destination: _____

Vessel Name: _____   LOA: _____

Type: _____   Size: _____   Tonnage: _____

Number of Days on Board: _____

Distance logged: _____

Night hours/watch: _____

Details of voyage: _____

Crew/Position/Weather/Special duties/Incidents:

_____

_____

_____

_____

Certifying Signature:
Captain or Owners Signature _____

Captain's Log ASA Documented Sailing Time

Dates   Leave: Arrive:

Times   Leave: Arrive:

Location   Origin:

Destination:

VesselName: LOA:

Type: Size: Tonnage:

Number of Days on Board:

Distance logged:

Night hours/watch:

Details of voyage:

Crew/Position/Weather/Special duties/Incidents:

_____

_____

_____

_____

Certifying Signature:
Captain or Owners Signature   _____

Captain's Log ASA Documented Sailing Time

Dates   Leave: Arrive:

Times   Leave: Arrive:

Location

Origin:

Destination:

Vessel Name: LOA:

Type: Size: Tonnage:

Number of Days on Board:

Distance logged:

Night hours/watch:

Details of voyage:

Crew/Position/Weather/Special duties/Incidents:

_____

_____

_____

_____

Certifying Signature:
Captain or Owners Signature   _____

Captain's Log ASA Documented Sailing Time

Dates   Leave: Arrive:

Times   Leave: Arrive:

Location   Origin:

                   Destination:

VesselName: LOA:

Type: Size: Tonnage:

Number of Days on Board:

Distance logged:

Night hours/watch:

Details of voyage:

Crew/Position/Weather/Special duties/Incidents:

_____

_____

_____

_____

_____

Certifying Signature:
Captain or Owners Signature   _____

Captain's Log ASA Documented Sailing Time

Dates   Leave: Arrive:

Times   Leave: Arrive:

Location
              Origin:

              Destination:

Vessel Name: LOA:

Type: Size: Tonnage:

Number of Days on Board:

Distance logged:

Night hours/watch:

Details of voyage:

Crew/Position/Weather/Special duties/Incidents:

_____

_____

_____

_____

Certifying Signature:
Captain or Owners Signature _____

Captain's Log ASA Documented Sailing Time

Dates   Leave: Arrive:

Times   Leave: Arrive:

Location   Origin:

        Destination:

Vessel Name: LOA:

Type: Size: Tonnage:

Number of Days on Board:

Distance logged:

Night hours/watch:

Details of voyage:

    Crew/Position/Weather/Special duties/Incidents:

_____

_____

_____

_____

_____

Certifying Signature:
Captain or Owners Signature _____

Captain's Log ASA Documented Sailing Time

Dates   Leave: Arrive:

Times   Leave: Arrive:

Location   Origin:

Destination:

VesselName: LOA:

Type: Size: Tonnage:

Number of Days on Board:

Distance logged:

Night hours/watch:

Details of voyage:

Crew/Position/Weather/Special duties/Incidents:

_____

_____

_____

_____

Certifying Signature:
Captain or Owners Signature _____

Captain's Log ASA Documented Sailing Time

Dates   Leave: Arrive:

Times   Leave: Arrive:

Location   Origin:

               Destination:

VesselName: LOA:

Type: Size: Tonnage:

Number of Days on Board:

Distance logged:

Night hours/watch:

Details of voyage:

            Crew/Position/Weather/Special duties/Incidents:

_____

_____

_____

_____

_____

Certifying Signature:
Captain or Owners Signature   _____

Captain's Log ASA Documented Sailing Time

Dates   Leave: Arrive:

Times   Leave: Arrive:

Location   Origin:

                   Destination:

VesselName: LOA:

Type: Size: Tonnage:

Number of Days on Board:

Distance logged:

Night hours/watch:

Details of voyage:

Crew/Position/Weather/Special duties/Incidents:

_____

_____

_____

_____

Certifying Signature:
Captain or Owners Signature _____

Captain's Log ASA Documented Sailing Time

Dates   Leave: Arrive:

Times   Leave: Arrive:

Location   Origin:

                              Destination:

VesselName: LOA:

Type: Size: Tonnage:

Number of Days on Board:

Distance logged:

Night hours/watch:

Details of voyage:

                    Crew/Position/Weather/Special duties/Incidents:

_____

_____

_____

_____

Certifying Signature:
Captain or Owners Signature   _____

Captain's Log ASA Documented Sailing Time

Dates   Leave: Arrive:

Times   Leave: Arrive:

Location   Origin:

                          Destination:

VesselName: LOA:

Type: Size: Tonnage:

Number of Days on Board:

Distance logged:

Night hours/watch:

Details of voyage:

Crew/Position/Weather/Special duties/Incidents:

_____

_____

_____

_____

Certifying Signature:
Captain or Owners Signature   _____

Captain's Log ASA Documented Sailing Time

Dates   Leave: Arrive:

Times   Leave: Arrive:

Location   Origin:

                      Destination:

VesselName: LOA:

Type: Size: Tonnage:

Number of Days on Board:

Distance logged:

Night hours/watch:

Details of voyage:

                      Crew/Position/Weather/Special duties/Incidents:

_____

_____

_____

_____

_____

Certifying Signature:
Captain or Owners Signature   _____

Captain's Log ASA Documented Sailing Time

Dates   Leave: Arrive:

Times   Leave: Arrive:

Location   Origin:

Destination:

VesselName: LOA:

Type: Size: Tonnage:

Number of Days on Board:

Distance logged:

Night hours/watch:

Details of voyage:

Crew/Position/Weather/Special duties/Incidents:

_____

_____

_____

_____

_____

Certifying Signature:
Captain or Owners Signature   _____

Captain's Log ASA Documented Sailing Time

Dates   Leave: Arrive:

Times   Leave: Arrive:

Location   Origin:

                    Destination:

VesselName: LOA:

Type: Size: Tonnage:

Number of Days on Board:

Distance logged:

Night hours/watch:

Details of voyage:

                    Crew/Position/Weather/Special duties/Incidents:

_____

_____

_____

_____

Certifying Signature:
Captain or Owners Signature   _____

Captain's Log ASA Documented Sailing Time

Dates   Leave: Arrive:

Times   Leave: Arrive:

Location   Origin:

               Destination:

Vessel Name: LOA:

Type: Size: Tonnage:

Number of Days on Board:

Distance logged:

Night hours/watch:

Details of voyage:

Crew/Position/Weather/Special duties/Incidents:

_____

_____

_____

_____

_____

Certifying Signature:
Captain or Owners Signature _____

Captain's Log ASA Documented Sailing Time

Dates   Leave: Arrive:

Times   Leave: Arrive:

Location   Origin:

                      Destination:

VesselName: LOA:

Type: Size: Tonnage:

Number of Days on Board:

Distance logged:

Night hours/watch:

Details of voyage:

Crew/Position/Weather/Special duties/Incidents:

_____

_____

_____

_____

Certifying Signature:

Captain or Owners Signature   _____

Captain's Log ASA Documented Sailing Time

Dates   Leave: Arrive:

Times   Leave: Arrive:

Location   Origin:

Destination:

VesselName: LOA:

Type: Size: Tonnage:

Number of Days on Board:

Distance logged:

Night hours/watch:

Details of voyage:

Crew/Position/Weather/Special duties/Incidents:

_____

_____

_____

_____

Certifying Signature:

Captain or Owners Signature   _____

Captain's Log ASA Documented Sailing Time

Dates   Leave: Arrive:

Times   Leave: Arrive:

Location   Origin:

Destination:

VesselName: LOA:

Type: Size: Tonnage:

Number of Days on Board:

Distance logged:

Night hours/watch:

Details of voyage:

Crew/Position/Weather/Special duties/Incidents:

_____

_____

_____

_____

Certifying Signature:
Captain or Owners Signature   _____

Captain's Log ASA Documented Sailing Time

Dates   Leave: Arrive:

Times   Leave: Arrive:

Location   Origin:

                    Destination:

Vessel Name: LOA:

Type: Size: Tonnage:

Number of Days on Board:

Distance logged:

Night hours/watch:

Details of voyage:

Crew/Position/Weather/Special duties/Incidents:

_____

_____

_____

_____

_____

Certifying Signature:
Captain or Owners Signature _____

Captain's Log ASA Documented Sailing Time

Dates   Leave: Arrive:

Times   Leave: Arrive:

Location   Origin:

                   Destination:

VesselName: LOA:

Type: Size: Tonnage:

Number of Days on Board:

Distance logged:

Night hours/watch:

Details of voyage:

Crew/Position/Weather/Special duties/Incidents:

_____

_____

_____

_____

_____

Certifying Signature:
Captain or Owners Signature   _____

Captain's Log ASA Documented Sailing Time

Dates   Leave: Arrive:

Times   Leave: Arrive:

Location   Origin:

                    Destination:

VesselName: LOA:

Type: Size: Tonnage:

Number of Days on Board:

Distance logged:

Night hours/watch:

Details of voyage:

Crew/Position/Weather/Special duties/Incidents:

_____

_____

_____

_____

Certifying Signature:
Captain or Owners Signature   _____

Captain's Log ASA Documented Sailing Time

Dates   Leave: Arrive:

Times   Leave: Arrive:

Location   Origin:

Destination:

VesselName: LOA:

Type: Size: Tonnage:

Number of Days on Board:

Distance logged:

Night hours/watch:

Details of voyage:

Crew/Position/Weather/Special duties/Incidents:

_____

_____

_____

_____

Certifying Signature:
Captain or Owners Signature   _____

Captain's Log ASA Documented Sailing Time

Dates   Leave: Arrive:

Times   Leave: Arrive:

Location   Origin:

                    Destination:

VesselName: LOA:

Type: Size: Tonnage:

Number of Days on Board:

Distance logged:

Night hours/watch:

Details of voyage:

Crew/Position/Weather/Special duties/Incidents:

_____

_____

_____

_____

Certifying Signature:
Captain or Owners Signature   _____

Captain's Log ASA Documented Sailing Time

Dates   Leave: Arrive:

Times   Leave: Arrive:

Location   Origin:

                  Destination:

VesselName: LOA:

Type: Size: Tonnage:

Number of Days on Board:

Distance logged:

Night hours/watch:

Details of voyage:

        Crew/Position/Weather/Special duties/Incidents:

_____

_____

_____

_____

_____

Certifying Signature:
Captain or Owners Signature _____

Captain's Log ASA Documented Sailing Time

Dates   Leave: Arrive:

Times   Leave: Arrive:

Location   Origin:

               Destination:

VesselName: LOA:

Type: Size: Tonnage:

Number of Days on Board:

Distance logged:

Night hours/watch:

Details of voyage:

             Crew/Position/Weather/Special duties/Incidents:

_____

_____

_____

_____

Certifying Signature:

Captain or Owners Signature   _____

Captain's Log ASA Documented Sailing Time

Dates   Leave: Arrive:

Times   Leave: Arrive:

Location   Origin:

                    Destination:

VesselName: LOA:

Type: Size: Tonnage:

Number of Days on Board:

Distance logged:

Night hours/watch:

Details of voyage:

Crew/Position/Weather/Special duties/Incidents:

_____

_____

_____

_____

Certifying Signature:
Captain or Owners Signature   _____

Captain's Log ASA Documented Sailing Time

Dates   Leave: Arrive:

Times   Leave: Arrive:

Location   Origin:

                    Destination:

VesselName: LOA:

Type: Size: Tonnage:

Number of Days on Board:

Distance logged:

Night hours/watch:

Details of voyage:

Crew/Position/Weather/Special duties/Incidents:

_____

_____

_____

_____

_____

Certifying Signature:
Captain or Owners Signature   _____

Captain's Log ASA Documented Sailing Time

Dates   Leave: Arrive:

Times   Leave: Arrive:

Location   Origin:

                 Destination:

VesselName: LOA:

Type: Size: Tonnage:

Number of Days on Board:

Distance logged:

Night hours/watch:

Details of voyage:

                 Crew/Position/Weather/Special duties/Incidents:

_____

_____

_____

_____

Certifying Signature:
Captain or Owners Signature   _____

Captain's Log ASA Documented Sailing Time

Dates   Leave: Arrive:

Times   Leave: Arrive:

Location   Origin:

                   Destination:

VesselName: LOA:

Type: Size: Tonnage:

Number of Days on Board:

Distance logged:

Night hours/watch:

Details of voyage:

                   Crew/Position/Weather/Special duties/Incidents:

_____

_____

_____

_____

_____

Certifying Signature:
Captain or Owners Signature   _____

Captain's Log ASA Documented Sailing Time

Dates   Leave: Arrive:

Times   Leave: Arrive:

Location   Origin:

                   Destination:

VesselName: LOA:

Type: Size: Tonnage:

Number of Days on Board:

Distance logged:

Night hours/watch:

Details of voyage:

                Crew/Position/Weather/Special duties/Incidents:

_____

_____

_____

_____

_____

Certifying Signature:
Captain or Owners Signature   _____

Captain's Log ASA Documented Sailing Time

Dates   Leave: Arrive:

Times   Leave: Arrive:

Location   Origin:

                        Destination:

VesselName: LOA:

Type: Size: Tonnage:

Number of Days on Board:

Distance logged:

Night hours/watch:

Details of voyage:

                   Crew/Position/Weather/Special duties/Incidents:

_____

_____

_____

_____

_____

Certifying Signature:
Captain or Owners Signature _____

Captain's Log ASA Documented Sailing Time

Dates   Leave: Arrive:

Times   Leave: Arrive:

Location   Origin:

Destination:

VesselName: LOA:

Type: Size: Tonnage:

Number of Days on Board:

Distance logged:

Night hours/watch:

Details of voyage:

Crew/Position/Weather/Special duties/Incidents:

_____

_____

_____

_____

_____

Certifying Signature:
Captain or Owners Signature   _____

Captain's Log ASA Documented Sailing Time

Dates   Leave: Arrive:

Times   Leave: Arrive:

Location   Origin:

                   Destination:

VesselName: LOA:

Type: Size: Tonnage:

Number of Days on Board:

Distance logged:

Night hours/watch:

Details of voyage:

                   Crew/Position/Weather/Special duties/Incidents:

_____

_____

_____

_____

Certifying Signature:
Captain or Owners Signature _____

Captain's Log ASA Documented Sailing Time

Dates   Leave: Arrive:

Times   Leave: Arrive:

Location   Origin:

Destination:

VesselName: LOA:

Type: Size: Tonnage:

Number of Days on Board:

Distance logged:

Night hours/watch:

Details of voyage:

Crew/Position/Weather/Special duties/Incidents:

_____

_____

_____

_____

Certifying Signature:
Captain or Owners Signature   _____

Captain's Log ASA Documented Sailing Time

Dates   Leave: Arrive:

Times   Leave: Arrive:

Location   Origin:

Destination:

VesselName: LOA:

Type: Size: Tonnage:

Number of Days on Board:

Distance logged:

Night hours/watch:

Details of voyage:

Crew/Position/Weather/Special duties/Incidents:

_____

_____

_____

_____

_____

Certifying Signature:
Captain or Owners Signature   _____

Captain's Log ASA Documented Sailing Time

Dates   Leave: Arrive:

Times   Leave: Arrive:

Location   Origin:

Destination:

VesselName: LOA:

Type: Size: Tonnage:

Number of Days on Board:

Distance logged:

Night hours/watch:

Details of voyage:

Crew/Position/Weather/Special duties/Incidents:

_____

_____

_____

_____

Certifying Signature:
Captain or Owners Signature   _____

Captain's Log ASA Documented Sailing Time

Dates   Leave: Arrive:

Times   Leave: Arrive:

Location   Origin:

                        Destination:

VesselName: LOA:

Type: Size: Tonnage:

Number of Days on Board:

Distance logged:

Night hours/watch:

Details of voyage:

Crew/Position/Weather/Special duties/Incidents:

_____

_____

_____

_____

_____

Certifying Signature:
Captain or Owners Signature   _____

Captain's Log ASA Documented Sailing Time

Dates   Leave: Arrive:

Times   Leave: Arrive:

Location   Origin:

                 Destination:

VesselName: LOA:

Type: Size: Tonnage:

Number of Days on Board:

Distance logged:

Night hours/watch:

Details of voyage:

        Crew/Position/Weather/Special duties/Incidents:

_____

_____

_____

_____

Certifying Signature:
Captain or Owners Signature _____

Captain's Log ASA Documented Sailing Time

Dates   Leave: Arrive:

Times   Leave: Arrive:

Location   Origin:

                 Destination:

VesselName: LOA:

Type: Size: Tonnage:

Number of Days on Board:

Distance logged:

Night hours/watch:

Details of voyage:

Crew/Position/Weather/Special duties/Incidents:

_____

_____

_____

_____

_____

Certifying Signature:
Captain or Owners Signature   _____

Captain's Log ASA Documented Sailing Time

Dates   Leave: Arrive:

Times   Leave: Arrive:

Location   Origin:

                      Destination:

VesselName: LOA:

Type: Size: Tonnage:

Number of Days on Board:

Distance logged:

Night hours/watch:

Details of voyage:

Crew/Position/Weather/Special duties/Incidents:

_____

_____

_____

_____

_____

Certifying Signature:
Captain or Owners Signature _____

Captain's Log ASA Documented Sailing Time

Dates   Leave: Arrive:

Times   Leave: Arrive:

Location   Origin:

                   Destination:

Vessel Name: LOA:

Type: Size: Tonnage:

Number of Days on Board:

Distance logged:

Night hours/watch:

Details of voyage:

Crew/Position/Weather/Special duties/Incidents:

_____

_____

_____

_____

Certifying Signature:
Captain or Owners Signature _____

Captain's Log ASA Documented Sailing Time

Dates   Leave: Arrive:

Times   Leave: Arrive:

Location   Origin:

                   Destination:

VesselName: LOA:

Type: Size: Tonnage:

Number of Days on Board:

Distance logged:

Night hours/watch:

Details of voyage:

                   Crew/Position/Weather/Special duties/Incidents:

_____

_____

_____

_____

Certifying Signature:
Captain or Owners Signature   _____

Captain's Log ASA Documented Sailing Time

Dates   Leave: Arrive:

Times   Leave: Arrive:

Location   Origin:

Destination:

VesselName: LOA:

Type: Size: Tonnage:

Number of Days on Board:

Distance logged:

Night hours/watch:

Details of voyage:

Crew/Position/Weather/Special duties/Incidents:

_____

_____

_____

_____

Certifying Signature:
Captain or Owners Signature   _____

Captain's Log ASA Documented Sailing Time

Dates   Leave: Arrive:

Times   Leave: Arrive:

Location   Origin:

                  Destination:

VesselName: LOA:

Type: Size: Tonnage:

Number of Days on Board:

Distance logged:

Night hours/watch:

Details of voyage:

                  Crew/Position/Weather/Special duties/Incidents:

_____

_____

_____

_____

_____

Certifying Signature:
Captain or Owners Signature   _____

Captain's Log ASA Documented Sailing Time

Dates   Leave: Arrive:

Times   Leave: Arrive:

Location   Origin:

Destination:

VesselName: LOA:

Type: Size: Tonnage:

Number of Days on Board:

Distance logged:

Night hours/watch:

Details of voyage:

Crew/Position/Weather/Special duties/Incidents:

_____

_____

_____

_____

Certifying Signature:
Captain or Owners Signature   _____

Captain's Log ASA Documented Sailing Time

Dates   Leave: Arrive:

Times   Leave: Arrive:

Location   Origin:

                 Destination:

VesselName: LOA:

Type: Size: Tonnage:

Number of Days on Board:

Distance logged:

Night hours/watch:

Details of voyage:

         Crew/Position/Weather/Special duties/Incidents:

_____

_____

_____

_____

Certifying Signature:
Captain or Owners Signature   _____

Captain's Log ASA Documented Sailing Time

Dates   Leave: Arrive:

Times   Leave: Arrive:

Location   Origin:

                   Destination:

VesselName: LOA:

Type: Size: Tonnage:

Number of Days on Board:

Distance logged:

Night hours/watch:

Details of voyage:

                   Crew/Position/Weather/Special duties/Incidents:

_____

_____

_____

_____

_____

Certifying Signature:
Captain or Owners Signature   _____

Captain's Log ASA Documented Sailing Time

Dates   Leave: Arrive:

Times   Leave: Arrive:

Location   Origin:

                    Destination:

VesselName: LOA:

Type: Size: Tonnage:

Number of Days on Board:

Distance logged:

Night hours/watch:

Details of voyage:

                    Crew/Position/Weather/Special duties/Incidents:

_____

_____

_____

_____

Certifying Signature:
Captain or Owners Signature _____

Captain's Log ASA Documented Sailing Time

Dates   Leave: Arrive:

Times   Leave: Arrive:

Location   Origin:

               Destination:

VesselName: LOA:

Type: Size: Tonnage:

Number of Days on Board:

Distance logged:

Night hours/watch:

Details of voyage:

Crew/Position/Weather/Special duties/Incidents:

_____

_____

_____

_____

Certifying Signature:
Captain or Owners Signature   _____

Captain's Log ASA Documented Sailing Time

Dates   Leave: Arrive:

Times   Leave: Arrive:

Location   Origin:

             Destination:

VesselName: LOA:

Type: Size: Tonnage:

Number of Days on Board:

Distance logged:

Night hours/watch:

Details of voyage:

        Crew/Position/Weather/Special duties/Incidents:

_____

_____

_____

_____

_____

Certifying Signature:
Captain or Owners Signature   _____

Captain's Log ASA Documented Sailing Time

Dates   Leave: Arrive:

Times   Leave: Arrive:

Location   Origin:

                Destination:

VesselName: LOA:

Type: Size: Tonnage:

Number of Days on Board:

Distance logged:

Night hours/watch:

Details of voyage:

               Crew/Position/Weather/Special duties/Incidents:

_____

_____

_____

_____

_____

Certifying Signature:
Captain or Owners Signature   _____

Captain's Log ASA Documented Sailing Time

Dates   Leave: Arrive:

Times   Leave: Arrive:

Location   Origin:

                    Destination:

VesselName: LOA:

Type: Size: Tonnage:

Number of Days on Board:

Distance logged:

Night hours/watch:

Details of voyage:

          Crew/Position/Weather/Special duties/Incidents:

_____

_____

_____

_____

_____

Certifying Signature:
Captain or Owners Signature   _____

Captain's Log ASA Documented Sailing Time

Dates   Leave: Arrive:

Times   Leave: Arrive:

Location   Origin:

Destination:

VesselName: LOA:

Type: Size: Tonnage:

Number of Days on Board:

Distance logged:

Night hours/watch:

Details of voyage:

Crew/Position/Weather/Special duties/Incidents:

_____

_____

_____

_____

_____

Certifying Signature:
Captain or Owners Signature _____

Captain's Log ASA Documented Sailing Time

Dates   Leave: Arrive:

Times   Leave: Arrive:

Location   Origin:

                    Destination:

VesselName: LOA:

Type: Size: Tonnage:

Number of Days on Board:

Distance logged:

Night hours/watch:

Details of voyage:

                    Crew/Position/Weather/Special duties/Incidents:

_____

_____

_____

_____

Certifying Signature:
Captain or Owners Signature   _____

Captain's Log ASA Documented Sailing Time

Dates   Leave: Arrive:

Times   Leave: Arrive:

Location   Origin:

               Destination:

VesselName: LOA:

Type: Size: Tonnage:

Number of Days on Board:

Distance logged:

Night hours/watch:

Details of voyage:

               Crew/Position/Weather/Special duties/Incidents:

_____

_____

_____

_____

Certifying Signature:
Captain or Owners Signature   _____

Captain's Log ASA Documented Sailing Time

Dates   Leave: Arrive:

Times   Leave: Arrive:

Location   Origin:

                        Destination:

VesselName: LOA:

Type: Size: Tonnage:

Number of Days on Board:

Distance logged:

Night hours/watch:

Details of voyage:

Crew/Position/Weather/Special duties/Incidents:

_____

_____

_____

_____

_____

Certifying Signature:
Captain or Owners Signature   _____

Captain's Log ASA Documented Sailing Time

Dates   Leave: Arrive:

Times   Leave: Arrive:

Location   Origin:

                       Destination:

VesselName: LOA:

Type: Size: Tonnage:

Number of Days on Board:

Distance logged:

Night hours/watch:

Details of voyage:

Crew/Position/Weather/Special duties/Incidents:

_____

_____

_____

_____

_____

Certifying Signature:
Captain or Owners Signature _____

Captain's Log ASA Documented Sailing Time

Dates   Leave: Arrive:

Times   Leave: Arrive:

Location   Origin:

                      Destination:

VesselName: LOA:

Type: Size: Tonnage:

Number of Days on Board:

Distance logged:

Night hours/watch:

Details of voyage:

Crew/Position/Weather/Special duties/Incidents:

_____

_____

_____

_____

Certifying Signature:
Captain or Owners Signature _____

Captain's Log ASA Documented Sailing Time

Dates   Leave: Arrive:

Times   Leave: Arrive:

Location   Origin:

                    Destination:

VesselName: LOA:

Type: Size: Tonnage:

Number of Days on Board:

Distance logged:

Night hours/watch:

Details of voyage:

                Crew/Position/Weather/Special duties/Incidents:

_____

_____

_____

_____

_____

Certifying Signature:
Captain or Owners Signature   _____

Captain's Log ASA Documented Sailing Time

Dates   Leave: Arrive:

Times   Leave: Arrive:

Location   Origin:

                   Destination:

VesselName: LOA:

Type: Size: Tonnage:

Number of Days on Board:

Distance logged:

Night hours/watch:

Details of voyage:

                   Crew/Position/Weather/Special duties/Incidents:

_____

_____

_____

_____

Certifying Signature:
Captain or Owners Signature   _____

Captain's Log ASA Documented Sailing Time

Dates   Leave: Arrive:

Times   Leave: Arrive:

Location   Origin:

                      Destination:

VesselName: LOA:

Type: Size: Tonnage:

Number of Days on Board:

Distance logged:

Night hours/watch:

Details of voyage:

              Crew/Position/Weather/Special duties/Incidents:

_____

_____

_____

_____

_____

Certifying Signature:
Captain or Owners Signature   _____

Captain's Log ASA Documented Sailing Time

Dates   Leave: Arrive:

Times   Leave: Arrive:

Location   Origin:

             Destination:

Vessel Name: LOA:

Type: Size: Tonnage:

Number of Days on Board:

Distance logged:

Night hours/watch:

Details of voyage:

Crew/Position/Weather/Special duties/Incidents:

_____

_____

_____

_____

Certifying Signature:
Captain or Owners Signature   _____

Captain's Log ASA Documented Sailing Time

Dates   Leave: Arrive:

Times   Leave: Arrive:

Location   Origin:

Destination:

VesselName: LOA:

Type: Size: Tonnage:

Number of Days on Board:

Distance logged:

Night hours/watch:

Details of voyage:

Crew/Position/Weather/Special duties/Incidents:

_____

_____

_____

_____

_____

Certifying Signature:
Captain or Owners Signature   _____

Captain's Log ASA Documented Sailing Time

Dates   Leave: Arrive:

Times   Leave: Arrive:

Location   Origin:

Destination:

VesselName: LOA:

Type: Size: Tonnage:

Number of Days on Board:

Distance logged:

Night hours/watch:

Details of voyage:

Crew/Position/Weather/Special duties/Incidents:

_____

_____

_____

_____

_____

Certifying Signature:
Captain or Owners Signature _____

Captain's Log ASA Documented Sailing Time

Dates   Leave: Arrive:

Times   Leave: Arrive:

Location   Origin:

                        Destination:

VesselName: LOA:

Type: Size: Tonnage:

Number of Days on Board:

Distance logged:

Night hours/watch:

Details of voyage:

Crew/Position/Weather/Special duties/Incidents:

_____

_____

_____

_____

Certifying Signature:
Captain or Owners Signature _____

Captain's Log ASA Documented Sailing Time

Dates   Leave: Arrive:

Times   Leave: Arrive:

Location   Origin:

Destination:

VesselName: LOA:

Type: Size: Tonnage:

Number of Days on Board:

Distance logged:

Night hours/watch:

Details of voyage:

Crew/Position/Weather/Special duties/Incidents:

_____

_____

_____

_____

Certifying Signature:
Captain or Owners Signature _____

Captain's Log ASA Documented Sailing Time

Dates   Leave: Arrive:

Times   Leave: Arrive:

Location   Origin:

                   Destination:

VesselName: LOA:

Type: Size: Tonnage:

Number of Days on Board:

Distance logged:

Night hours/watch:

Details of voyage:

Crew/Position/Weather/Special duties/Incidents:

_____

_____

_____

_____

_____

Certifying Signature:

Captain or Owners Signature   _____

Captain's Log ASA Documented Sailing Time

Dates Leave: Arrive:

Times Leave: Arrive:

Location Origin:

Destination:

VesselName: LOA:

Type: Size: Tonnage:

Number of Days on Board:

Distance logged:

Night hours/watch:

Details of voyage:

Crew/Position/Weather/Special duties/Incidents:

_____

_____

_____

_____

Certifying Signature:
Captain or Owners Signature   _____

Captain's Log ASA Documented Sailing Time

Dates   Leave: Arrive:

Times   Leave: Arrive:

Location   Origin:

                   Destination:

VesselName: LOA:

Type: Size: Tonnage:

Number of Days on Board:

Distance logged:

Night hours/watch:

Details of voyage:

Crew/Position/Weather/Special duties/Incidents:

_____

_____

_____

_____

Certifying Signature:

Captain or Owners Signature _____

Captain's Log ASA Documented Sailing Time

Dates   Leave: Arrive:

Times   Leave: Arrive:

Location   Origin:

                   Destination:

VesselName: LOA:

Type: Size: Tonnage:

Number of Days on Board:

Distance logged:

Night hours/watch:

Details of voyage:

Crew/Position/Weather/Special duties/Incidents:

_____

_____

_____

_____

Certifying Signature:
Captain or Owners Signature _____

Captain's Log ASA Documented Sailing Time

Dates   Leave: Arrive:

Times   Leave: Arrive:

Location   Origin:

                   Destination:

VesselName: LOA:

Type: Size: Tonnage:

Number of Days on Board:

Distance logged:

Night hours/watch:

Details of voyage:

Crew/Position/Weather/Special duties/Incidents:

_____

_____

_____

_____

Certifying Signature:
Captain or Owners Signature   _____

Captain's Log ASA Documented Sailing Time

Dates   Leave: Arrive:

Times   Leave: Arrive:

Location   Origin:

Destination:

VesselName: LOA:

Type: Size: Tonnage:

Number of Days on Board:

Distance logged:

Night hours/watch:

Details of voyage:

Crew/Position/Weather/Special duties/Incidents:

_____

_____

_____

_____

Certifying Signature:
Captain or Owners Signature _____

Captain's Log ASA Documented Sailing Time

Dates   Leave: Arrive:

Times   Leave: Arrive:

Location   Origin:

Destination:

VesselName: LOA:

Type: Size: Tonnage:

Number of Days on Board:

Distance logged:

Night hours/watch:

Details of voyage:

Crew/Position/Weather/Special duties/Incidents:

_____

_____

_____

_____

Certifying Signature:
Captain or Owners Signature   _____

Captain's Log ASA Documented Sailing Time

Dates   Leave: Arrive:

Times   Leave: Arrive:

Location   Origin:

                     Destination:

VesselName: LOA:

Type: Size: Tonnage:

Number of Days on Board:

Distance logged:

Night hours/watch:

Details of voyage:

Crew/Position/Weather/Special duties/Incidents:

_____

_____

_____

_____

_____

Certifying Signature:
Captain or Owners Signature   _____

Captain's Log ASA Documented Sailing Time

Dates   Leave: Arrive:

Times   Leave: Arrive:

Location   Origin:

   Destination:

VesselName: LOA:

Type: Size: Tonnage:

Number of Days on Board:

Distance logged:

Night hours/watch:

Details of voyage:

Crew/Position/Weather/Special duties/Incidents:

_____

_____

_____

_____

Certifying Signature:
Captain or Owners Signature _____

Captain's Log ASA Documented Sailing Time

Dates   Leave: Arrive:

Times   Leave: Arrive:

Location   Origin:

        Destination:

VesselName: LOA:

Type: Size: Tonnage:

Number of Days on Board:

Distance logged:

Night hours/watch:

Details of voyage:

        Crew/Position/Weather/Special duties/Incidents:

_____

_____

_____

_____

Certifying Signature:
Captain or Owners Signature   _____

Captain's Log ASA Documented Sailing Time

Dates   Leave: Arrive:

Times   Leave: Arrive:

Location   Origin:

Destination:

VesselName: LOA:

Type: Size: Tonnage:

Number of Days on Board:

Distance logged:

Night hours/watch:

Details of voyage:

Crew/Position/Weather/Special duties/Incidents:

_____

_____

_____

_____

_____

Certifying Signature:
Captain or Owners Signature   _____

Captain's Log ASA Documented Sailing Time

Dates   Leave: Arrive:

Times   Leave: Arrive:

Location   Origin:

                    Destination:

VesselName: LOA:

Type: Size: Tonnage:

Number of Days on Board:

Distance logged:

Night hours/watch:

Details of voyage:

                    Crew/Position/Weather/Special duties/Incidents:

_____

_____

_____

_____

Certifying Signature:
Captain or Owners Signature   _____

Captain's Log ASA Documented Sailing Time

Dates   Leave: Arrive:

Times   Leave: Arrive:

Location   Origin:

                   Destination:

VesselName: LOA:

Type: Size: Tonnage:

Number of Days on Board:

Distance logged:

Night hours/watch:

Details of voyage:

Crew/Position/Weather/Special duties/Incidents:

_____

_____

_____

_____

Certifying Signature:

Captain or Owners Signature   _____

Captain's Log ASA Documented Sailing Time

Dates   Leave: Arrive:

Times   Leave: Arrive:

Location   Origin:

                   Destination:

VesselName: LOA:

Type: Size: Tonnage:

Number of Days on Board:

Distance logged:

Night hours/watch:

Details of voyage:

Crew/Position/Weather/Special duties/Incidents:

_____

_____

_____

_____

_____

Certifying Signature:
Captain or Owners Signature   _____

Captain's Log ASA Documented Sailing Time

Dates   Leave: Arrive:

Times   Leave: Arrive:

Location   Origin:

                   Destination:

VesselName: LOA:

Type: Size: Tonnage:

Number of Days on Board:

Distance logged:

Night hours/watch:

Details of voyage:

        Crew/Position/Weather/Special duties/Incidents:

_____

_____

_____

_____

Certifying Signature:
Captain or Owners Signature   _____

Captain's Log ASA Documented Sailing Time

Dates   Leave: Arrive:

Times   Leave: Arrive:

Location   Origin:

                     Destination:

VesselName: LOA:

Type: Size: Tonnage:

Number of Days on Board:

Distance logged:

Night hours/watch:

Details of voyage:

              Crew/Position/Weather/Special duties/Incidents:

_____

_____

_____

_____

Certifying Signature:
Captain or Owners Signature _____

Captain's Log ASA Documented Sailing Time

Dates   Leave: Arrive:

Times   Leave: Arrive:

Location   Origin:

                   Destination:

VesselName: LOA:

Type: Size: Tonnage:

Number of Days on Board:

Distance logged:

Night hours/watch:

Details of voyage:

Crew/Position/Weather/Special duties/Incidents:

_____

_____

_____

_____

Certifying Signature:
Captain or Owners Signature _____

Captain's Log ASA Documented Sailing Time

Dates   Leave: Arrive:

Times   Leave: Arrive:

Location   Origin:

Destination:

VesselName: LOA:

Type: Size: Tonnage:

Number of Days on Board:

Distance logged:

Night hours/watch:

Details of voyage:

Crew/Position/Weather/Special duties/Incidents:

_____

_____

_____

_____

_____

Certifying Signature:
Captain or Owners Signature   _____

Captain's Log ASA Documented Sailing Time

Dates   Leave: Arrive:

Times   Leave: Arrive:

Location   Origin:

                 Destination:

VesselName: LOA:

Type: Size: Tonnage:

Number of Days on Board:

Distance logged:

Night hours/watch:

Details of voyage:

Crew/Position/Weather/Special duties/Incidents:

_____

_____

_____

_____

Certifying Signature:
Captain or Owners Signature   _____

Captain's Log ASA Documented Sailing Time

Dates   Leave: Arrive:

Times   Leave: Arrive:

Location   Origin:

                    Destination:

VesselName: LOA:

Type: Size: Tonnage:

Number of Days on Board:

Distance logged:

Night hours/watch:

Details of voyage:

Crew/Position/Weather/Special duties/Incidents:

_____

_____

_____

_____

Certifying Signature:
Captain or Owners Signature   _____

Captain's Log ASA Documented Sailing Time

Dates   Leave: Arrive:

Times   Leave: Arrive:

Location   Origin:

                      Destination:

VesselName: LOA:

Type: Size: Tonnage:

Number of Days on Board:

Distance logged:

Night hours/watch:

Details of voyage:

          Crew/Position/Weather/Special duties/Incidents:

_____

_____

_____

_____

Certifying Signature:
Captain or Owners Signature _____

Captain's Log ASA Documented Sailing Time

Dates   Leave: Arrive:

Times   Leave: Arrive:

Location   Origin:

Destination:

VesselName: LOA:

Type: Size: Tonnage:

Number of Days on Board:

Distance logged:

Night hours/watch:

Details of voyage:

Crew/Position/Weather/Special duties/Incidents:

_____

_____

_____

_____

Certifying Signature:
Captain or Owners Signature _____

Captain's Log ASA Documented Sailing Time

Dates   Leave: Arrive:

Times   Leave: Arrive:

Location   Origin:

                   Destination:

VesselName: LOA:

Type: Size: Tonnage:

Number of Days on Board:

Distance logged:

Night hours/watch:

Details of voyage:

Crew/Position/Weather/Special duties/Incidents:

_____

_____

_____

_____

Certifying Signature:
Captain or Owners Signature _____

Captain's Log ASA Documented Sailing Time

Dates   Leave: Arrive:

Times   Leave: Arrive:

Location   Origin:

                      Destination:

VesselName: LOA:

Type: Size: Tonnage:

Number of Days on Board:

Distance logged:

Night hours/watch:

Details of voyage:

Crew/Position/Weather/Special duties/Incidents:

_____

_____

_____

_____

Certifying Signature:
Captain or Owners Signature _____

Captain's Log ASA Documented Sailing Time

Dates   Leave: Arrive:

Times   Leave: Arrive:

Location   Origin:

Destination:

VesselName: LOA:

Type: Size: Tonnage:

Number of Days on Board:

Distance logged:

Night hours/watch:

Details of voyage:

Crew/Position/Weather/Special duties/Incidents:

_____

_____

_____

_____

Certifying Signature:
Captain or Owners Signature _____

Captain's Log ASA Documented Sailing Time

Dates   Leave: Arrive:

Times   Leave: Arrive:

Location   Origin:

          Destination:

VesselName: LOA:

Type: Size: Tonnage:

Number of Days on Board:

Distance logged:

Night hours/watch:

Details of voyage:

Crew/Position/Weather/Special duties/Incidents:

_____

_____

_____

_____

Certifying Signature:

Captain or Owners Signature   _____

Captain's Log ASA Documented Sailing Time

Dates   Leave: Arrive:

Times   Leave: Arrive:

Location   Origin:

                    Destination:

VesselName: LOA:

Type: Size: Tonnage:

Number of Days on Board:

Distance logged:

Night hours/watch:

Details of voyage:

Crew/Position/Weather/Special duties/Incidents:

_____

_____

_____

_____

_____

Certifying Signature:
Captain or Owners Signature _____

Captain's Log ASA Documented Sailing Time

Dates   Leave: Arrive:

Times   Leave: Arrive:

Location   Origin:

                     Destination:

VesselName: LOA:

Type: Size: Tonnage:

Number of Days on Board:

Distance logged:

Night hours/watch:

Details of voyage:

Crew/Position/Weather/Special duties/Incidents:

_____

_____

_____

_____

_____

Certifying Signature:
Captain or Owners Signature   _____

Captain's Log ASA Documented Sailing Time

Dates   Leave: Arrive:

Times   Leave: Arrive:

Location   Origin:

               Destination:

VesselName: LOA:

Type: Size: Tonnage:

Number of Days on Board:

Distance logged:

Night hours/watch:

Details of voyage:

Crew/Position/Weather/Special duties/Incidents:

_____

_____

_____

_____

_____

Certifying Signature:

Captain or Owners Signature   _____

Captain's Log ASA Documented Sailing Time

Dates   Leave: Arrive:

Times   Leave: Arrive:

Location   Origin:

                       Destination:

VesselName: LOA:

Type: Size: Tonnage:

Number of Days on Board:

Distance logged:

Night hours/watch:

Details of voyage:

                    Crew/Position/Weather/Special duties/Incidents:

_____

_____

_____

_____

_____

Certifying Signature:
Captain or Owners Signature   _____

Captain's Log ASA Documented Sailing Time

Dates   Leave: Arrive:

Times   Leave: Arrive:

Location   Origin:

Destination:

VesselName: LOA:

Type: Size: Tonnage:

Number of Days on Board:

Distance logged:

Night hours/watch:

Details of voyage:

Crew/Position/Weather/Special duties/Incidents:

_____

_____

_____

_____

Certifying Signature:

Captain or Owners Signature _____

Captain's Log ASA Documented Sailing Time

Dates   Leave: Arrive:

Times   Leave: Arrive:

Location   Origin:

                 Destination:

VesselName: LOA:

Type: Size: Tonnage:

Number of Days on Board:

Distance logged:

Night hours/watch:

Details of voyage:

         Crew/Position/Weather/Special duties/Incidents:

_____

_____

_____

_____

Certifying Signature:
Captain or Owners Signature   _____

Captain's Log ASA Documented Sailing Time

Dates   Leave: Arrive:

Times   Leave: Arrive:

Location   Origin:

              Destination:

VesselName: LOA:

Type: Size: Tonnage:

Number of Days on Board:

Distance logged:

Night hours/watch:

Details of voyage:

         Crew/Position/Weather/Special duties/Incidents:

_____

_____

_____

_____

Certifying Signature:

Captain or Owners Signature _____

Captain's Log ASA Documented Sailing Time

Dates   Leave: Arrive:

Times   Leave: Arrive:

Location   Origin:

                    Destination:

VesselName: LOA:

Type: Size: Tonnage:

Number of Days on Board:

Distance logged:

Night hours/watch:

Details of voyage:

Crew/Position/Weather/Special duties/Incidents:

_____

_____

_____

_____

Certifying Signature:
Captain or Owners Signature   _____

Captain's Log ASA Documented Sailing Time

Dates   Leave: Arrive:

Times   Leave: Arrive:

Location   Origin:

                    Destination:

VesselName: LOA:

Type: Size: Tonnage:

Number of Days on Board:

Distance logged:

Night hours/watch:

Details of voyage:

                    Crew/Position/Weather/Special duties/Incidents:

_____

_____

_____

_____

_____

Certifying Signature:
Captain or Owners Signature   _____

Captain's Log ASA Documented Sailing Time

Dates   Leave: Arrive:

Times   Leave: Arrive:

Location   Origin:

                   Destination:

VesselName: LOA:

Type: Size: Tonnage:

Number of Days on Board:

Distance logged:

Night hours/watch:

Details of voyage:

Crew/Position/Weather/Special duties/Incidents:

_____

_____

_____

_____

_____

Certifying Signature:
Captain or Owners Signature _____

Captain's Log ASA Documented Sailing Time

Dates   Leave: Arrive:

Times   Leave: Arrive:

Location   Origin:

                   Destination:

VesselName: LOA:

Type: Size: Tonnage:

Number of Days on Board:

Distance logged:

Night hours/watch:

Details of voyage:

Crew/Position/Weather/Special duties/Incidents:

_____

_____

_____

_____

Certifying Signature:
Captain or Owners Signature _____

Captain's Log ASA Documented Sailing Time

Dates   Leave: Arrive:

Times   Leave: Arrive:

Location   Origin:

                   Destination:

VesselName: LOA:

Type: Size: Tonnage:

Number of Days on Board:

Distance logged:

Night hours/watch:

Details of voyage:

Crew/Position/Weather/Special duties/Incidents:

_____

_____

_____

_____

_____

Certifying Signature:
Captain or Owners Signature   _____

Captain's Log ASA Documented Sailing Time

Dates   Leave: Arrive:

Times   Leave: Arrive:

Location   Origin:

                   Destination:

VesselName: LOA:

Type: Size: Tonnage:

Number of Days on Board:

Distance logged:

Night hours/watch:

Details of voyage:

                   Crew/Position/Weather/Special duties/Incidents:

_____

_____

_____

_____

Certifying Signature:
Captain or Owners Signature   _____

Captain's Log ASA Documented Sailing Time

Dates   Leave: Arrive:

Times   Leave: Arrive:

Location   Origin:

                   Destination:

VesselName: LOA:

Type: Size: Tonnage:

Number of Days on Board:

Distance logged:

Night hours/watch:

Details of voyage:

                 Crew/Position/Weather/Special duties/Incidents:

_____

_____

_____

_____

Certifying Signature:
Captain or Owners Signature   _____

Captain's Log ASA Documented Sailing Time

Dates   Leave: Arrive:

Times   Leave: Arrive:

Location   Origin:

                              Destination:

VesselName: LOA:

Type: Size: Tonnage:

Number of Days on Board:

Distance logged:

Night hours/watch:

Details of voyage:

Crew/Position/Weather/Special duties/Incidents:

_____

_____

_____

_____

Certifying Signature:
Captain or Owners Signature _____

Captain's Log ASA Documented Sailing Time

Dates   Leave: Arrive:

Times   Leave: Arrive:

Location   Origin:

               Destination:

VesselName: LOA:

Type: Size: Tonnage:

Number of Days on Board:

Distance logged:

Night hours/watch:

Details of voyage:

             Crew/Position/Weather/Special duties/Incidents:

_____

_____

_____

_____

Certifying Signature:
Captain or Owners Signature   _____

Captain's Log ASA Documented Sailing Time

Dates   Leave: Arrive:

Times   Leave: Arrive:

Location   Origin:

Destination:

VesselName: LOA:

Type: Size: Tonnage:

Number of Days on Board:

Distance logged:

Night hours/watch:

Details of voyage:

Crew/Position/Weather/Special duties/Incidents:

_____

_____

_____

_____

_____

Certifying Signature:
Captain or Owners Signature   _____

Captain's Log ASA Documented Sailing Time

Dates   Leave: Arrive:

Times   Leave: Arrive:

Location   Origin:

Destination:

VesselName: LOA:

Type: Size: Tonnage:

Number of Days on Board:

Distance logged:

Night hours/watch:

Details of voyage:

Crew/Position/Weather/Special duties/Incidents:

_____

_____

_____

_____

Certifying Signature:
Captain or Owners Signature   _____

Captain's Log ASA Documented Sailing Time

Dates   Leave: Arrive:

Times   Leave: Arrive:

Location   Origin:

                 Destination:

VesselName: LOA:

Type: Size: Tonnage:

Number of Days on Board:

Distance logged:

Night hours/watch:

Details of voyage:

            Crew/Position/Weather/Special duties/Incidents:

_____

_____

_____

_____

_____

Certifying Signature:
Captain or Owners Signature _____

Captain's Log ASA Documented Sailing Time

Dates   Leave: Arrive:

Times   Leave: Arrive:

Location   Origin:

Destination:

VesselName: LOA:

Type: Size: Tonnage:

Number of Days on Board:

Distance logged:

Night hours/watch:

Details of voyage:

Crew/Position/Weather/Special duties/Incidents:

_____

_____

_____

_____

Certifying Signature:
Captain or Owners Signature   _____

Captain's Log ASA Documented Sailing Time

Dates   Leave: Arrive:

Times   Leave: Arrive:

Location   Origin:

                      Destination:

VesselName: LOA:

Type: Size: Tonnage:

Number of Days on Board:

Distance logged:

Night hours/watch:

Details of voyage:

Crew/Position/Weather/Special duties/Incidents:

_____

_____

_____

_____

_____

Certifying Signature:
Captain or Owners Signature   _____

Captain's Log ASA Documented Sailing Time

Dates   Leave: Arrive:

Times   Leave: Arrive:

Location   Origin:

                         Destination:

VesselName: LOA:

Type: Size: Tonnage:

Number of Days on Board:

Distance logged:

Night hours/watch:

Details of voyage:

               Crew/Position/Weather/Special duties/Incidents:

_____

_____

_____

_____

Certifying Signature:
Captain or Owners Signature   _____

Captain's Log ASA Documented Sailing Time

Dates   Leave: Arrive:

Times   Leave: Arrive:

Location   Origin:

                   Destination:

VesselName: LOA:

Type: Size: Tonnage:

Number of Days on Board:

Distance logged:

Night hours/watch:

Details of voyage:

                   Crew/Position/Weather/Special duties/Incidents:

_____

_____

_____

_____

Certifying Signature:
Captain or Owners Signature _____

Captain's Log ASA Documented Sailing Time

Dates   Leave: Arrive:

Times   Leave: Arrive:

Location   Origin:

                        Destination:

VesselName: LOA:

Type: Size: Tonnage:

Number of Days on Board:

Distance logged:

Night hours/watch:

Details of voyage:

                Crew/Position/Weather/Special duties/Incidents:

_____

_____

_____

_____

_____

Certifying Signature:
Captain or Owners Signature _____

Captain's Log ASA Documented Sailing Time

Dates   Leave: Arrive:

Times   Leave: Arrive:

Location   Origin:

                Destination:

VesselName: LOA:

Type: Size: Tonnage:

Number of Days on Board:

Distance logged:

Night hours/watch:

Details of voyage:

                Crew/Position/Weather/Special duties/Incidents:

_____

_____

_____

_____

_____

Certifying Signature:
Captain or Owners Signature   _____

Captain's Log ASA Documented Sailing Time

Dates   Leave: Arrive:

Times   Leave: Arrive:

Location   Origin:

Destination:

VesselName: LOA:

Type: Size: Tonnage:

Number of Days on Board:

Distance logged:

Night hours/watch:

Details of voyage:

Crew/Position/Weather/Special duties/Incidents:

_____

_____

_____

_____

Certifying Signature:
Captain or Owners Signature   _____

Captain's Log ASA Documented Sailing Time

Dates   Leave: Arrive:

Times   Leave: Arrive:

Location   Origin:

                   Destination:

VesselName: LOA:

Type: Size: Tonnage:

Number of Days on Board:

Distance logged:

Night hours/watch:

Details of voyage:

            Crew/Position/Weather/Special duties/Incidents:

_____

_____

_____

_____

Certifying Signature:
Captain or Owners Signature   _____

Captain's Log ASA Documented Sailing Time

Dates   Leave: Arrive:

Times   Leave: Arrive:

Location   Origin:

Destination:

VesselName: LOA:

Type: Size: Tonnage:

Number of Days on Board:

Distance logged:

Night hours/watch:

Details of voyage:

Crew/Position/Weather/Special duties/Incidents:

_____

_____

_____

_____

Certifying Signature:
Captain or Owners Signature   _____

Captain's Log ASA Documented Sailing Time

Dates   Leave: Arrive:

Times   Leave: Arrive:

Location   Origin:

                   Destination:

VesselName: LOA:

Type: Size: Tonnage:

Number of Days on Board:

Distance logged:

Night hours/watch:

Details of voyage:

Crew/Position/Weather/Special duties/Incidents:

_____

_____

_____

_____

_____

Certifying Signature:
Captain or Owners Signature _____

Captain's Log ASA Documented Sailing Time

Dates   Leave: Arrive:

Times   Leave: Arrive:

Location   Origin:

                    Destination:

VesselName: LOA:

Type: Size: Tonnage:

Number of Days on Board:

Distance logged:

Night hours/watch:

Details of voyage:

Crew/Position/Weather/Special duties/Incidents:

_____

_____

_____

_____

Certifying Signature:
Captain or Owners Signature   _____

Captain's Log ASA Documented Sailing Time

Dates   Leave: Arrive:

Times   Leave: Arrive:

Location   Origin:

                   Destination:

VesselName: LOA:

Type: Size: Tonnage:

Number of Days on Board:

Distance logged:

Night hours/watch:

Details of voyage:

                   Crew/Position/Weather/Special duties/Incidents:

_____

_____

_____

_____

_____

Certifying Signature:
Captain or Owners Signature _____

Captain's Log ASA Documented Sailing Time

Dates   Leave: Arrive:

Times   Leave: Arrive:

Location   Origin:

            Destination:

VesselName: LOA:

Type: Size: Tonnage:

Number of Days on Board:

Distance logged:

Night hours/watch:

Details of voyage:

            Crew/Position/Weather/Special duties/Incidents:

_____

_____

_____

_____

Certifying Signature:
Captain or Owners Signature   _____

Captain's Log ASA Documented Sailing Time

Dates   Leave: Arrive:

Times   Leave: Arrive:

Location   Origin:

                          Destination:

VesselName: LOA:

Type: Size: Tonnage:

Number of Days on Board:

Distance logged:

Night hours/watch:

Details of voyage:

                    Crew/Position/Weather/Special duties/Incidents:

_____

_____

_____

_____

Certifying Signature:
Captain or Owners Signature   _____

Captain's Log ASA Documented Sailing Time

Dates   Leave: Arrive:

Times   Leave: Arrive:

Location   Origin:

Destination:

VesselName: LOA:

Type: Size: Tonnage:

Number of Days on Board:

Distance logged:

Night hours/watch:

Details of voyage:

Crew/Position/Weather/Special duties/Incidents:

_____

_____

_____

_____

Certifying Signature:
Captain or Owners Signature _____

Captain's Log ASA Documented Sailing Time

Dates   Leave: Arrive:

Times   Leave: Arrive:

Location   Origin:

Destination:

VesselName: LOA:

Type: Size: Tonnage:

Number of Days on Board:

Distance logged:

Night hours/watch:

Details of voyage:

Crew/Position/Weather/Special duties/Incidents:

_____

_____

_____

_____

_____

Certifying Signature:
Captain or Owners Signature   _____

Captain's Log ASA Documented Sailing Time

Dates   Leave: Arrive:

Times   Leave: Arrive:

Location   Origin:

                   Destination:

VesselName: LOA:

Type: Size: Tonnage:

Number of Days on Board:

Distance logged:

Night hours/watch:

Details of voyage:

Crew/Position/Weather/Special duties/Incidents:

_____

_____

_____

_____

_____

Certifying Signature:
Captain or Owners Signature _____

Captain's Log ASA Documented Sailing Time

Dates   Leave: Arrive:

Times   Leave: Arrive:

Location   Origin:

                   Destination:

VesselName: LOA:

Type: Size: Tonnage:

Number of Days on Board:

Distance logged:

Night hours/watch:

Details of voyage:

                Crew/Position/Weather/Special duties/Incidents:

_____

_____

_____

_____

_____

Certifying Signature:
Captain or Owners Signature _____

Captain's Log ASA Documented Sailing Time

Dates   Leave: Arrive:

Times   Leave: Arrive:

Location   Origin:

Destination:

VesselName: LOA:

Type: Size: Tonnage:

Number of Days on Board:

Distance logged:

Night hours/watch:

Details of voyage:

Crew/Position/Weather/Special duties/Incidents:

_____

_____

_____

_____

Certifying Signature:
Captain or Owners Signature   _____

Captain's Log ASA Documented Sailing Time

Dates   Leave: Arrive:

Times   Leave: Arrive:

Location   Origin:

                        Destination:

VesselName: LOA:

Type: Size: Tonnage:

Number of Days on Board:

Distance logged:

Night hours/watch:

Details of voyage:

Crew/Position/Weather/Special duties/Incidents:

_____

_____

_____

_____

_____

Certifying Signature:
Captain or Owners Signature _____

Captain's Log ASA Documented Sailing Time

Dates   Leave: Arrive:

Times   Leave: Arrive:

Location   Origin:

                        Destination:

VesselName: LOA:

Type: Size: Tonnage:

Number of Days on Board:

Distance logged:

Night hours/watch:

Details of voyage:

                Crew/Position/Weather/Special duties/Incidents:

_____

_____

_____

_____

Certifying Signature:
Captain or Owners Signature   _____

Captain's Log ASA Documented Sailing Time

Dates   Leave: Arrive:

Times   Leave: Arrive:

Location   Origin:

                    Destination:

VesselName: LOA:

Type: Size: Tonnage:

Number of Days on Board:

Distance logged:

Night hours/watch:

Details of voyage:

               Crew/Position/Weather/Special duties/Incidents:

_____

_____

_____

_____

_____

Certifying Signature:
Captain or Owners Signature   _____

Captain's Log ASA Documented Sailing Time

Dates   Leave: Arrive:

Times   Leave: Arrive:

Location   Origin:

                 Destination:

VesselName: LOA:

Type: Size: Tonnage:

Number of Days on Board:

Distance logged:

Night hours/watch:

Details of voyage:

        Crew/Position/Weather/Special duties/Incidents:

_____

_____

_____

_____

_____

Certifying Signature:
Captain or Owners Signature   _____

Captain's Log ASA Documented Sailing Time

Dates   Leave: Arrive:

Times   Leave: Arrive:

Location   Origin:

Destination:

Vessel Name: LOA:

Type: Size: Tonnage:

Number of Days on Board:

Distance logged:

Night hours/watch:

Details of voyage:

Crew/Position/Weather/Special duties/Incidents:

_____

_____

_____

_____

_____

Certifying Signature:
Captain or Owners Signature _____

Captain's Log ASA Documented Sailing Time

Dates   Leave: Arrive:

Times   Leave: Arrive:

Location   Origin:

                        Destination:

VesselName: LOA:

Type: Size: Tonnage:

Number of Days on Board:

Distance logged:

Night hours/watch:

Details of voyage:

            Crew/Position/Weather/Special duties/Incidents:

_____

_____

_____

_____

Certifying Signature:
Captain or Owners Signature   _____

Captain's Log ASA Documented Sailing Time

Dates   Leave: Arrive:

Times   Leave: Arrive:

Location   Origin:

                        Destination:

VesselName: LOA:

Type: Size: Tonnage:

Number of Days on Board:

Distance logged:

Night hours/watch:

Details of voyage:

                Crew/Position/Weather/Special duties/Incidents:

_____

_____

_____

_____

Certifying Signature:
Captain or Owners Signature   _____

Captain's Log ASA Documented Sailing Time

Dates   Leave: Arrive:

Times   Leave: Arrive:

Location   Origin:

                   Destination:

VesselName: LOA:

Type: Size: Tonnage:

Number of Days on Board:

Distance logged:

Night hours/watch:

Details of voyage:

Crew/Position/Weather/Special duties/Incidents:

_____

_____

_____

_____

Certifying Signature:
Captain or Owners Signature   _____

Captain's Log ASA Documented Sailing Time

Dates   Leave: Arrive:

Times   Leave: Arrive:

Location   Origin:

                    Destination:

VesselName: LOA:

Type: Size: Tonnage:

Number of Days on Board:

Distance logged:

Night hours/watch:

Details of voyage:

                    Crew/Position/Weather/Special duties/Incidents:

_____

_____

_____

_____

_____

Certifying Signature:
Captain or Owners Signature   _____

Captain's Log ASA Documented Sailing Time

Dates   Leave: Arrive:

Times   Leave: Arrive:

Location   Origin:

       Destination:

VesselName: LOA:

Type: Size: Tonnage:

Number of Days on Board:

Distance logged:

Night hours/watch:

Details of voyage:

    Crew/Position/Weather/Special duties/Incidents:

_____

_____

_____

_____

_____

Certifying Signature:
Captain or Owners Signature _____

Captain's Log ASA Documented Sailing Time

Dates   Leave: Arrive:

Times   Leave: Arrive:

Location   Origin:

                   Destination:

VesselName: LOA:

Type: Size: Tonnage:

Number of Days on Board:

Distance logged:

Night hours/watch:

Details of voyage:

Crew/Position/Weather/Special duties/Incidents:

_____

_____

_____

_____

Certifying Signature:
Captain or Owners Signature   _____

Captain's Log ASA Documented Sailing Time

Dates Leave: _____ Arrive: _____

Times Leave: _____ Arrive: _____

Location Origin: _____

Destination: _____

VesselName: _____ LOA: _____

Type: _____ Size: _____ Tonnage: _____

Number of Days on Board: _____

Distance logged: _____

Night hours/watch: _____

Details of voyage: _____

Crew/Position/Weather/Special duties/Incidents:

_____

_____

_____

_____

Certifying Signature:
Captain or Owners Signature _____

Captain's Log ASA Documented Sailing Time

Dates   Leave: Arrive:

Times   Leave: Arrive:

Location   Origin:

                          Destination:

VesselName: LOA:

Type: Size: Tonnage:

Number of Days on Board:

Distance logged:

Night hours/watch:

Details of voyage:

                Crew/Position/Weather/Special duties/Incidents:

_____

_____

_____

_____

Certifying Signature:
Captain or Owners Signature   _____

Captain's Log ASA Documented Sailing Time

Dates   Leave: Arrive:

Times   Leave: Arrive:

Location   Origin:

                   Destination:

VesselName: LOA:

Type: Size: Tonnage:

Number of Days on Board:

Distance logged:

Night hours/watch:

Details of voyage:

Crew/Position/Weather/Special duties/Incidents:

_____

_____

_____

_____

Certifying Signature:
Captain or Owners Signature   _____

Captain's Log ASA Documented Sailing Time

Dates   Leave: Arrive:

Times   Leave: Arrive:

Location   Origin:

                   Destination:

VesselName: LOA:

Type: Size: Tonnage:

Number of Days on Board:

Distance logged:

Night hours/watch:

Details of voyage:

Crew/Position/Weather/Special duties/Incidents:

_____

_____

_____

_____

Certifying Signature:

Captain or Owners Signature _____

Captain's Log ASA Documented Sailing Time

Dates   Leave: Arrive:

Times   Leave: Arrive:

Location   Origin:

                     Destination:

Vessel Name: LOA:

Type: Size: Tonnage:

Number of Days on Board:

Distance logged:

Night hours/watch:

Details of voyage:

Crew/Position/Weather/Special duties/Incidents:

_____

_____

_____

_____

Certifying Signature:
Captain or Owners Signature _____

Captain's Log ASA Documented Sailing Time

Dates   Leave: Arrive:

Times   Leave: Arrive:

Location   Origin:

                    Destination:

VesselName: LOA:

Type: Size: Tonnage:

Number of Days on Board:

Distance logged:

Night hours/watch:

Details of voyage:

                    Crew/Position/Weather/Special duties/Incidents:

_____

_____

_____

_____

_____

Certifying Signature:
Captain or Owners Signature   _____

Captain's Log ASA Documented Sailing Time

Dates   Leave: Arrive:

Times   Leave: Arrive:

Location   Origin:

Destination:

VesselName: LOA:

Type: Size: Tonnage:

Number of Days on Board:

Distance logged:

Night hours/watch:

Details of voyage:

Crew/Position/Weather/Special duties/Incidents:

_____

_____

_____

_____

_____

Certifying Signature:
Captain or Owners Signature   _____

Captain's Log ASA Documented Sailing Time

Dates   Leave: Arrive:

Times   Leave: Arrive:

Location   Origin:

Destination:

VesselName: LOA:

Type: Size: Tonnage:

Number of Days on Board:

Distance logged:

Night hours/watch:

Details of voyage:

Crew/Position/Weather/Special duties/Incidents:

_____

_____

_____

_____

_____

Certifying Signature:
Captain or Owners Signature _____

Captain's Log ASA Documented Sailing Time

Dates   Leave: Arrive:

Times   Leave: Arrive:

Location   Origin:

                     Destination:

VesselName: LOA:

Type: Size: Tonnage:

Number of Days on Board:

Distance logged:

Night hours/watch:

Details of voyage:

Crew/Position/Weather/Special duties/Incidents:

_____

_____

_____

_____

Certifying Signature:
Captain or Owners Signature _____

Captain's Log ASA Documented Sailing Time

Dates   Leave: Arrive:

Times   Leave: Arrive:

Location   Origin:

                    Destination:

VesselName: LOA:

Type: Size: Tonnage:

Number of Days on Board:

Distance logged:

Night hours/watch:

Details of voyage:

Crew/Position/Weather/Special duties/Incidents:

_____

_____

_____

_____

_____

Certifying Signature:
Captain or Owners Signature _____

Captain's Log ASA Documented Sailing Time

Dates   Leave: Arrive:

Times   Leave: Arrive:

Location   Origin:

                 Destination:

Vessel Name: LOA:

Type: Size: Tonnage:

Number of Days on Board:

Distance logged:

Night hours/watch:

Details of voyage:

Crew/Position/Weather/Special duties/Incidents:

_____

_____

_____

_____

Certifying Signature:
Captain or Owners Signature   _____

Captain's Log ASA Documented Sailing Time

Dates   Leave: Arrive:

Times   Leave: Arrive:

Location   Origin:

                Destination:

VesselName: LOA:

Type: Size: Tonnage:

Number of Days on Board:

Distance logged:

Night hours/watch:

Details of voyage:

Crew/Position/Weather/Special duties/Incidents:

_____

_____

_____

_____

_____

Certifying Signature:
Captain or Owners Signature   _____

Captain's Log ASA Documented Sailing Time

Dates   Leave: Arrive:

Times   Leave: Arrive:

Location   Origin:

                   Destination:

VesselName: LOA:

Type: Size: Tonnage:

Number of Days on Board:

Distance logged:

Night hours/watch:

Details of voyage:

Crew/Position/Weather/Special duties/Incidents:

_____

_____

_____

_____

Certifying Signature:
Captain or Owners Signature _____

Captain's Log ASA Documented Sailing Time

Dates   Leave: Arrive:

Times   Leave: Arrive:

Location   Origin:

                 Destination:

VesselName: LOA:

Type: Size: Tonnage:

Number of Days on Board:

Distance logged:

Night hours/watch:

Details of voyage:

                 Crew/Position/Weather/Special duties/Incidents:

_____

_____

_____

_____

Certifying Signature:
Captain or Owners Signature   _____

Captain's Log ASA Documented Sailing Time

Dates   Leave: Arrive:

Times   Leave: Arrive:

Location   Origin:

                    Destination:

VesselName: LOA:

Type: Size: Tonnage:

Number of Days on Board:

Distance logged:

Night hours/watch:

Details of voyage:

Crew/Position/Weather/Special duties/Incidents:

_____

_____

_____

_____

Certifying Signature:
Captain or Owners Signature   _____

Captain's Log ASA Documented Sailing Time

Dates   Leave: Arrive:

Times   Leave: Arrive:

Location   Origin:

                   Destination:

VesselName: LOA:

Type: Size: Tonnage:

Number of Days on Board:

Distance logged:

Night hours/watch:

Details of voyage:

                   Crew/Position/Weather/Special duties/Incidents:

_____

_____

_____

_____

Certifying Signature:
Captain or Owners Signature   _____

Captain's Log ASA Documented Sailing Time

Dates   Leave: Arrive:

Times   Leave: Arrive:

Location   Origin:

                  Destination:

VesselName: LOA:

Type: Size: Tonnage:

Number of Days on Board:

Distance logged:

Night hours/watch:

Details of voyage:

Crew/Position/Weather/Special duties/Incidents:

_____

_____

_____

_____

Certifying Signature:
Captain or Owners Signature _____

Captain's Log ASA Documented Sailing Time

Dates   Leave: Arrive:

Times   Leave: Arrive:

Location   Origin:

                    Destination:

VesselName: LOA:

Type: Size: Tonnage:

Number of Days on Board:

Distance logged:

Night hours/watch:

Details of voyage:

Crew/Position/Weather/Special duties/Incidents:

_____

_____

_____

_____

_____

Certifying Signature:
Captain or Owners Signature _____

Captain's Log ASA Documented Sailing Time

Dates   Leave: Arrive:

Times   Leave: Arrive:

Location   Origin:

                Destination:

VesselName: LOA:

Type: Size: Tonnage:

Number of Days on Board:

Distance logged:

Night hours/watch:

Details of voyage:

Crew/Position/Weather/Special duties/Incidents:

_____

_____

_____

_____

Certifying Signature:
Captain or Owners Signature   _____

Captain's Log ASA Documented Sailing Time

Dates   Leave: Arrive:

Times   Leave: Arrive:

Location   Origin:

                     Destination:

VesselName: LOA:

Type: Size: Tonnage:

Number of Days on Board:

Distance logged:

Night hours/watch:

Details of voyage:

                 Crew/Position/Weather/Special duties/Incidents:

_____

_____

_____

_____

_____

Certifying Signature:
Captain or Owners Signature   _____

Captain's Log ASA Documented Sailing Time

Dates   Leave: Arrive:

Times   Leave: Arrive:

Location   Origin:

                          Destination:

VesselName: LOA:

Type: Size: Tonnage:

Number of Days on Board:

Distance logged:

Night hours/watch:

Details of voyage:

Crew/Position/Weather/Special duties/Incidents:

_____

_____

_____

_____

Certifying Signature:
Captain or Owners Signature   _____

Captain's Log ASA Documented Sailing Time

Dates   Leave: Arrive:

Times   Leave: Arrive:

Location   Origin:

                      Destination:

VesselName: LOA:

Type: Size: Tonnage:

Number of Days on Board:

Distance logged:

Night hours/watch:

Details of voyage:

Crew/Position/Weather/Special duties/Incidents:

_____

_____

_____

_____

_____

Certifying Signature:
Captain or Owners Signature   _____

Captain's Log ASA Documented Sailing Time

Dates   Leave: Arrive:

Times   Leave: Arrive:

Location   Origin:

                   Destination:

VesselName: LOA:

Type: Size: Tonnage:

Number of Days on Board:

Distance logged:

Night hours/watch:

Details of voyage:

Crew/Position/Weather/Special duties/Incidents:

_____

_____

_____

_____

Certifying Signature:
Captain or Owners Signature   _____

Captain's Log ASA Documented Sailing Time

Dates   Leave: Arrive:

Times   Leave: Arrive:

Location   Origin:

                     Destination:

VesselName: LOA:

Type: Size: Tonnage:

Number of Days on Board:

Distance logged:

Night hours/watch:

Details of voyage:

Crew/Position/Weather/Special duties/Incidents:

_____

_____

_____

_____

Certifying Signature:
Captain or Owners Signature   _____

Captain's Log ASA Documented Sailing Time

Dates   Leave: Arrive:

Times   Leave: Arrive:

Location   Origin:

                          Destination:

VesselName: LOA:

Type: Size: Tonnage:

Number of Days on Board:

Distance logged:

Night hours/watch:

Details of voyage:

Crew/Position/Weather/Special duties/Incidents:

_____

_____

_____

_____

Certifying Signature:
Captain or Owners Signature _____

Captain's Log ASA Documented Sailing Time

Dates   Leave: Arrive:

Times   Leave: Arrive:

Location   Origin:

Destination:

VesselName: LOA:

Type: Size: Tonnage:

Number of Days on Board:

Distance logged:

Night hours/watch:

Details of voyage:

Crew/Position/Weather/Special duties/Incidents:

_____

_____

_____

_____

_____

Certifying Signature:
Captain or Owners Signature _____

Captain's Log ASA Documented Sailing Time

Dates   Leave: Arrive:

Times   Leave: Arrive:

Location   Origin:

                         Destination:

VesselName: LOA:

Type: Size: Tonnage:

Number of Days on Board:

Distance logged:

Night hours/watch:

Details of voyage:

Crew/Position/Weather/Special duties/Incidents:

_____

_____

_____

_____

Certifying Signature:
Captain or Owners Signature _____

Captain's Log ASA Documented Sailing Time

Dates   Leave: Arrive:

Times   Leave: Arrive:

Location   Origin:

                 Destination:

VesselName: LOA:

Type: Size: Tonnage:

Number of Days on Board:

Distance logged:

Night hours/watch:

Details of voyage:

Crew/Position/Weather/Special duties/Incidents:

_____

_____

_____

_____

Certifying Signature:
Captain or Owners Signature _____

Captain's Log ASA Documented Sailing Time

Dates   Leave: Arrive:

Times   Leave: Arrive:

Location   Origin:

Destination:

VesselName: LOA:

Type: Size: Tonnage:

Number of Days on Board:

Distance logged:

Night hours/watch:

Details of voyage:

Crew/Position/Weather/Special duties/Incidents:

_____

_____

_____

Certifying Signature:
Captain or Owners Signature   _____

Captain's Log ASA Documented Sailing Time

Dates   Leave: Arrive:

Times   Leave: Arrive:

Location
Origin:

Destination:

VesselName: LOA:

Type: Size: Tonnage:

Number of Days on Board:

Distance logged:

Night hours/watch:

Details of voyage:

Crew/Position/Weather/Special duties/Incidents:

_____

_____

_____

_____

_____

Certifying Signature:
Captain or Owners Signature _____

Captain's Log ASA Documented Sailing Time

Dates   Leave: Arrive:

Times   Leave: Arrive:

Location   Origin:

Destination:

VesselName: LOA:

Type: Size: Tonnage:

Number of Days on Board:

Distance logged:

Night hours/watch:

Details of voyage:

Crew/Position/Weather/Special duties/Incidents:

_____

_____

_____

_____

Certifying Signature:
Captain or Owners Signature _____

Captain's Log ASA Documented Sailing Time

Dates   Leave: Arrive:

Times   Leave: Arrive:

Location   Origin:

Destination:

VesselName: LOA:

Type: Size: Tonnage:

Number of Days on Board:

Distance logged:

Night hours/watch:

Details of voyage:

Crew/Position/Weather/Special duties/Incidents:

_____

_____

_____

_____

Certifying Signature:
Captain or Owners Signature   _____

Captain's Log ASA Documented Sailing Time

Dates   Leave: Arrive:

Times   Leave: Arrive:

Location   Origin:

          Destination:

VesselName: LOA:

Type: Size: Tonnage:

Number of Days on Board:

Distance logged:

Night hours/watch:

Details of voyage:

          Crew/Position/Weather/Special duties/Incidents:

_____

_____

_____

_____

Certifying Signature:
Captain or Owners Signature   _____

Captain's Log ASA Documented Sailing Time

Dates   Leave: Arrive:

Times   Leave: Arrive:

Location   Origin:

                      Destination:

VesselName: LOA:

Type: Size: Tonnage:

Number of Days on Board:

Distance logged:

Night hours/watch:

Details of voyage:

Crew/Position/Weather/Special duties/Incidents:

_____

_____

_____

_____

Certifying Signature:
Captain or Owners Signature   _____

Captain's Log ASA Documented Sailing Time

Dates   Leave: Arrive:

Times   Leave: Arrive:

Location   Origin:

                   Destination:

VesselName: LOA:

Type: Size: Tonnage:

Number of Days on Board:

Distance logged:

Night hours/watch:

Details of voyage:

Crew/Position/Weather/Special duties/Incidents:

_____

_____

_____

_____

Certifying Signature:
Captain or Owners Signature   _____

Captain's Log ASA Documented Sailing Time

Dates   Leave: Arrive:

Times   Leave: Arrive:

Location   Origin:

                  Destination:

VesselName: LOA:

Type: Size: Tonnage:

Number of Days on Board:

Distance logged:

Night hours/watch:

Details of voyage:

Crew/Position/Weather/Special duties/Incidents:

_____

_____

_____

_____

Certifying Signature:
Captain or Owners Signature _____

Captain's Log ASA Documented Sailing Time

Dates   Leave: Arrive:

Times   Leave: Arrive:

Location   Origin:

Destination:

VesselName: LOA:

Type: Size: Tonnage:

Number of Days on Board:

Distance logged:

Night hours/watch:

Details of voyage:

Crew/Position/Weather/Special duties/Incidents:

_____

_____

_____

_____

Certifying Signature:
Captain or Owners Signature _____

Captain's Log ASA Documented Sailing Time

Dates   Leave: Arrive:

Times   Leave: Arrive:

Location   Origin:

            Destination:

VesselName: LOA:

Type: Size: Tonnage:

Number of Days on Board:

Distance logged:

Night hours/watch:

Details of voyage:

        Crew/Position/Weather/Special duties/Incidents:

_____

_____

_____

_____

_____

Certifying Signature:
Captain or Owners Signature   _____

Captain's Log ASA Documented Sailing Time

Dates   Leave: Arrive:

Times   Leave: Arrive:

Location   Origin:

                        Destination:

VesselName: LOA:

Type: Size: Tonnage:

Number of Days on Board:

Distance logged:

Night hours/watch:

Details of voyage:

Crew/Position/Weather/Special duties/Incidents:

_____

_____

_____

_____

Certifying Signature:
Captain or Owners Signature _____

Captain's Log ASA Documented Sailing Time

Dates   Leave: Arrive:

Times   Leave: Arrive:

Location   Origin:

Destination:

Vessel Name: LOA:

Type: Size: Tonnage:

Number of Days on Board:

Distance logged:

Night hours/watch:

Details of voyage:

Crew/Position/Weather/Special duties/Incidents:

_____

_____

_____

_____

_____

Certifying Signature:
Captain or Owners Signature   _____

Captain's Log ASA Documented Sailing Time

Dates   Leave: Arrive:

Times   Leave: Arrive:

Location   Origin:

                   Destination:

VesselName: LOA:

Type: Size: Tonnage:

Number of Days on Board:

Distance logged:

Night hours/watch:

Details of voyage:

Crew/Position/Weather/Special duties/Incidents:

_____

_____

_____

_____

Certifying Signature:
Captain or Owners Signature _____

Captain's Log ASA Documented Sailing Time

Dates   Leave: Arrive:

Times   Leave: Arrive:

Location   Origin:

                Destination:

VesselName: LOA:

Type: Size: Tonnage:

Number of Days on Board:

Distance logged:

Night hours/watch:

Details of voyage:

                Crew/Position/Weather/Special duties/Incidents:

_____

_____

_____

_____

_____

Certifying Signature:
Captain or Owners Signature   _____

Captain's Log ASA Documented Sailing Time

Dates   Leave: Arrive:

Times   Leave: Arrive:

Location   Origin:

Destination:

VesselName: LOA:

Type: Size: Tonnage:

Number of Days on Board:

Distance logged:

Night hours/watch:

Details of voyage:

Crew/Position/Weather/Special duties/Incidents:

_____

_____

_____

_____

Certifying Signature:
Captain or Owners Signature   _____

Captain's Log ASA Documented Sailing Time

Dates   Leave: Arrive:

Times   Leave: Arrive:

Location
              Origin:

              Destination:

VesselName: LOA:

Type: Size: Tonnage:

Number of Days on Board:

Distance logged:

Night hours/watch:

Details of voyage:

                    Crew/Position/Weather/Special duties/Incidents:

_____

_____

_____

_____

Certifying Signature:
Captain or Owners Signature   _____

Captain's Log ASA Documented Sailing Time

Dates   Leave: Arrive:

Times   Leave: Arrive:

Location   Origin:

                        Destination:

VesselName: LOA:

Type: Size: Tonnage:

Number of Days on Board:

Distance logged:

Night hours/watch:

Details of voyage:

                Crew/Position/Weather/Special duties/Incidents:

_____

_____

_____

_____

Certifying Signature:
Captain or Owners Signature   _____

Captain's Log ASA Documented Sailing Time

Dates   Leave: Arrive:

Times   Leave: Arrive:

Location   Origin:

                   Destination:

VesselName: LOA:

Type: Size: Tonnage:

Number of Days on Board:

Distance logged:

Night hours/watch:

Details of voyage:

Crew/Position/Weather/Special duties/Incidents:

_____

_____

_____

_____

_____

Certifying Signature:
Captain or Owners Signature   _____

Captain's Log ASA Documented Sailing Time

Dates   Leave: Arrive:

Times   Leave: Arrive:

Location   Origin:

                   Destination:

VesselName: LOA:

Type: Size: Tonnage:

Number of Days on Board:

Distance logged:

Night hours/watch:

Details of voyage:

                   Crew/Position/Weather/Special duties/Incidents:

_____

_____

_____

_____

Certifying Signature:
Captain or Owners Signature   _____

Captain's Log ASA Documented Sailing Time

Dates   Leave: Arrive:

Times   Leave: Arrive:

Location   Origin:

                    Destination:

VesselName: LOA:

Type: Size: Tonnage:

Number of Days on Board:

Distance logged:

Night hours/watch:

Details of voyage:

Crew/Position/Weather/Special duties/Incidents:

_____

_____

_____

_____

Certifying Signature:
Captain or Owners Signature   _____

Captain's Log ASA Documented Sailing Time

Dates   Leave: Arrive:

Times   Leave: Arrive:

Location   Origin:

Destination:

VesselName: LOA:

Type: Size: Tonnage:

Number of Days on Board:

Distance logged:

Night hours/watch:

Details of voyage:

Crew/Position/Weather/Special duties/Incidents:

_____

_____

_____

_____

Certifying Signature:
Captain or Owners Signature   _____

Captain's Log ASA Documented Sailing Time

Dates   Leave: Arrive:

Times   Leave: Arrive:

Location   Origin:

                Destination:

VesselName: LOA:

Type: Size: Tonnage:

Number of Days on Board:

Distance logged:

Night hours/watch:

Details of voyage:

            Crew/Position/Weather/Special duties/Incidents:

_____

_____

_____

_____

_____

Certifying Signature:
Captain or Owners Signature _____

Captain's Log ASA Documented Sailing Time

Dates   Leave: Arrive:

Times   Leave: Arrive:

Location   Origin:

                   Destination:

VesselName: LOA:

Type: Size: Tonnage:

Number of Days on Board:

Distance logged:

Night hours/watch:

Details of voyage:

                   Crew/Position/Weather/Special duties/Incidents:

_____

_____

_____

_____

Certifying Signature:
Captain or Owners Signature   _____

Captain's Log ASA Documented Sailing Time

Dates   Leave: Arrive:

Times   Leave: Arrive:

Location   Origin:

                Destination:

VesselName: LOA:

Type: Size: Tonnage:

Number of Days on Board:

Distance logged:

Night hours/watch:

Details of voyage:

                Crew/Position/Weather/Special duties/Incidents:

_____

_____

_____

_____

Certifying Signature:
Captain or Owners Signature _____

Captain's Log ASA Documented Sailing Time

Dates   Leave: Arrive:

Times   Leave: Arrive:

Location   Origin:

                   Destination:

VesselName: LOA:

Type: Size: Tonnage:

Number of Days on Board:

Distance logged:

Night hours/watch:

Details of voyage:

Crew/Position/Weather/Special duties/Incidents:

_____

_____

_____

_____

Certifying Signature:
Captain or Owners Signature _____

Captain's Log ASA Documented Sailing Time

Dates   Leave: Arrive:

Times   Leave: Arrive:

Location   Origin:

                   Destination:

VesselName: LOA:

Type: Size: Tonnage:

Number of Days on Board:

Distance logged:

Night hours/watch:

Details of voyage:

Crew/Position/Weather/Special duties/Incidents:

_____

_____

_____

_____

_____

Certifying Signature:
Captain or Owners Signature _____

Captain's Log ASA Documented Sailing Time

Dates   Leave: Arrive:

Times   Leave: Arrive:

Location   Origin:

                    Destination:

VesselName: LOA:

Type: Size: Tonnage:

Number of Days on Board:

Distance logged:

Night hours/watch:

Details of voyage:

                    Crew/Position/Weather/Special duties/Incidents:

_____

_____

_____

_____

_____

Certifying Signature:
Captain or Owners Signature _____

Captain's Log ASA Documented Sailing Time

Dates   Leave: Arrive:

Times   Leave: Arrive:

Location   Origin:

                   Destination:

VesselName: LOA:

Type: Size: Tonnage:

Number of Days on Board:

Distance logged:

Night hours/watch:

Details of voyage:

Crew/Position/Weather/Special duties/Incidents:

_____

_____

_____

_____

Certifying Signature:
Captain or Owners Signature   _____

Captain's Log ASA Documented Sailing Time

Dates   Leave: Arrive:

Times   Leave: Arrive:

Location   Origin:

Destination:

VesselName: LOA:

Type: Size: Tonnage:

Number of Days on Board:

Distance logged:

Night hours/watch:

Details of voyage:

Crew/Position/Weather/Special duties/Incidents:

_____

_____

_____

_____

Certifying Signature:
Captain or Owners Signature   _____

Captain's Log ASA Documented Sailing Time

Dates   Leave: Arrive:

Times   Leave: Arrive:

Location   Origin:

Destination:

VesselName: LOA:

Type: Size: Tonnage:

Number of Days on Board:

Distance logged:

Night hours/watch:

Details of voyage:

Crew/Position/Weather/Special duties/Incidents:

_____

_____

_____

_____

_____

Certifying Signature:
Captain or Owners Signature   _____

Captain's Log ASA Documented Sailing Time

Dates   Leave: Arrive:

Times   Leave: Arrive:

Location   Origin:

                   Destination:

VesselName: LOA:

Type: Size: Tonnage:

Number of Days on Board:

Distance logged:

Night hours/watch:

Details of voyage:

Crew/Position/Weather/Special duties/Incidents:

_____

_____

_____

_____

Certifying Signature:
Captain or Owners Signature _____

Captain's Log ASA Documented Sailing Time

Dates   Leave: Arrive:

Times   Leave: Arrive:

Location   Origin:

             Destination:

VesselName: LOA:

Type: Size: Tonnage:

Number of Days on Board:

Distance logged:

Night hours/watch:

Details of voyage:

          Crew/Position/Weather/Special duties/Incidents:

_____

_____

_____

_____

_____

Certifying Signature:
Captain or Owners Signature   _____

Captain's Log ASA Documented Sailing Time

Dates   Leave: Arrive:

Times   Leave: Arrive:

Location   Origin:

             Destination:

VesselName: LOA:

Type: Size: Tonnage:

Number of Days on Board:

Distance logged:

Night hours/watch:

Details of voyage:

         Crew/Position/Weather/Special duties/Incidents:

_____

_____

_____

_____

_____

Certifying Signature:
Captain or Owners Signature   _____

Captain's Log ASA Documented Sailing Time

Dates   Leave: Arrive:

Times   Leave: Arrive:

Location   Origin:

Destination:

Vessel Name: LOA:

Type: Size: Tonnage:

Number of Days on Board:

Distance logged:

Night hours/watch:

Details of voyage:

Crew/Position/Weather/Special duties/Incidents:

_____

_____

_____

_____

_____

Certifying Signature:
Captain or Owners Signature   _____

Captain's Log ASA Documented Sailing Time

Dates   Leave: Arrive:

Times   Leave: Arrive:

Location   Origin:

                         Destination:

VesselName: LOA:

Type: Size: Tonnage:

Number of Days on Board:

Distance logged:

Night hours/watch:

Details of voyage:

Crew/Position/Weather/Special duties/Incidents:

_____

_____

_____

_____

Certifying Signature:
Captain or Owners Signature _____

Captain's Log ASA Documented Sailing Time

Dates   Leave: Arrive:

Times   Leave: Arrive:

Location   Origin:

Destination:

VesselName: LOA:

Type: Size: Tonnage:

Number of Days on Board:

Distance logged:

Night hours/watch:

Details of voyage:

Crew/Position/Weather/Special duties/Incidents:

_____

_____

_____

_____

Certifying Signature:
Captain or Owners Signature _____

Captain's Log ASA Documented Sailing Time

Dates   Leave: Arrive:

Times   Leave: Arrive:

Location   Origin:

                    Destination:

Vessel Name: LOA:

Type: Size: Tonnage:

Number of Days on Board:

Distance logged:

Night hours/watch:

Details of voyage:

Crew/Position/Weather/Special duties/Incidents:

_____

_____

_____

_____

Certifying Signature:
Captain or Owners Signature   _____

Captain's Log ASA Documented Sailing Time

Dates   Leave: Arrive:

Times   Leave: Arrive:

Location   Origin:

                     Destination:

VesselName: LOA:

Type: Size: Tonnage:

Number of Days on Board:

Distance logged:

Night hours/watch:

Details of voyage:

                Crew/Position/Weather/Special duties/Incidents:

_____

_____

_____

_____

_____

Certifying Signature:
Captain or Owners Signature   _____

Captain's Log ASA Documented Sailing Time

Dates   Leave: Arrive:

Times   Leave: Arrive:

Location   Origin:

                    Destination:

VesselName: LOA:

Type: Size: Tonnage:

Number of Days on Board:

Distance logged:

Night hours/watch:

Details of voyage:

                    Crew/Position/Weather/Special duties/Incidents:

_____

_____

_____

_____

Certifying Signature:
Captain or Owners Signature   _____

Captain's Log ASA Documented Sailing Time

Dates   Leave: Arrive:

Times   Leave: Arrive:

Location   Origin:

                    Destination:

VesselName: LOA:

Type: Size: Tonnage:

Number of Days on Board:

Distance logged:

Night hours/watch:

Details of voyage:

                    Crew/Position/Weather/Special duties/Incidents:

_____

_____

_____

_____

_____

Certifying Signature:
Captain or Owners Signature   _____

Captain's Log ASA Documented Sailing Time

Dates   Leave: Arrive:

Times   Leave: Arrive:

Location   Origin:

                   Destination:

VesselName: LOA:

Type: Size: Tonnage:

Number of Days on Board:

Distance logged:

Night hours/watch:

Details of voyage:

Crew/Position/Weather/Special duties/Incidents:

_____

_____

_____

_____

Certifying Signature:
Captain or Owners Signature   _____

Captain's Log ASA Documented Sailing Time

Dates   Leave: Arrive:

Times   Leave: Arrive:

Location   Origin:

Destination:

VesselName: LOA:

Type: Size: Tonnage:

Number of Days on Board:

Distance logged:

Night hours/watch:

Details of voyage:

Crew/Position/Weather/Special duties/Incidents:

_____

_____

_____

_____

Certifying Signature:
Captain or Owners Signature   _____

Captain's Log ASA Documented Sailing Time

Dates   Leave: Arrive:

Times   Leave: Arrive:

Location   Origin:

                   Destination:

VesselName: LOA:

Type: Size: Tonnage:

Number of Days on Board:

Distance logged:

Night hours/watch:

Details of voyage:

Crew/Position/Weather/Special duties/Incidents:

_____

_____

_____

_____

Certifying Signature:
Captain or Owners Signature   _____

Captain's Log ASA Documented Sailing Time

Dates   Leave: Arrive:

Times   Leave: Arrive:

Location   Origin:

Destination:

VesselName: LOA:

Type: Size: Tonnage:

Number of Days on Board:

Distance logged:

Night hours/watch:

Details of voyage:

Crew/Position/Weather/Special duties/Incidents:

_____

_____

_____

_____

Certifying Signature:
Captain or Owners Signature _____

Captain's Log ASA Documented Sailing Time

Dates   Leave: Arrive:

Times   Leave: Arrive:

Location   Origin:

                        Destination:

VesselName: LOA:

Type: Size: Tonnage:

Number of Days on Board:

Distance logged:

Night hours/watch:

Details of voyage:

Crew/Position/Weather/Special duties/Incidents:

_____

_____

_____

_____

Certifying Signature:
Captain or Owners Signature _____

Captain's Log ASA Documented Sailing Time

Dates   Leave: Arrive:

Times   Leave: Arrive:

Location   Origin:

                   Destination:

Vessel Name: LOA:

Type: Size: Tonnage:

Number of Days on Board:

Distance logged:

Night hours/watch:

Details of voyage:

Crew/Position/Weather/Special duties/Incidents:

_____

_____

_____

_____

_____

Certifying Signature:
Captain or Owners Signature _____

Captain's Log ASA Documented Sailing Time

Dates   Leave: Arrive:

Times   Leave: Arrive:

Location   Origin:

                   Destination:

VesselName: LOA:

Type: Size: Tonnage:

Number of Days on Board:

Distance logged:

Night hours/watch:

Details of voyage:

                Crew/Position/Weather/Special duties/Incidents:

_____

_____

_____

_____

Certifying Signature:
Captain or Owners Signature   _____

Captain's Log ASA Documented Sailing Time

Dates   Leave: Arrive:

Times   Leave: Arrive:

Location   Origin:

          Destination:

VesselName: LOA:

Type: Size: Tonnage:

Number of Days on Board:

Distance logged:

Night hours/watch:

Details of voyage:

          Crew/Position/Weather/Special duties/Incidents:

_____

_____

_____

_____

Certifying Signature:
Captain or Owners Signature   _____

Captain's Log ASA Documented Sailing Time

Dates   Leave: Arrive:

Times   Leave: Arrive:

Location   Origin:

                    Destination:

VesselName: LOA:

Type: Size: Tonnage:

Number of Days on Board:

Distance logged:

Night hours/watch:

Details of voyage:

Crew/Position/Weather/Special duties/Incidents:

_____

_____

_____

_____

Certifying Signature:
Captain or Owners Signature   _____

Captain's Log ASA Documented Sailing Time

Dates   Leave: Arrive:

Times   Leave: Arrive:

Location   Origin:

                        Destination:

VesselName: LOA:

Type: Size: Tonnage:

Number of Days on Board:

Distance logged:

Night hours/watch:

Details of voyage:

Crew/Position/Weather/Special duties/Incidents:

_____

_____

_____

_____

_____

Certifying Signature:
Captain or Owners Signature _____

Captain's Log ASA Documented Sailing Time

Dates   Leave: Arrive:

Times   Leave: Arrive:

Location   Origin:

                   Destination:

VesselName: LOA:

Type: Size: Tonnage:

Number of Days on Board:

Distance logged:

Night hours/watch:

Details of voyage:

Crew/Position/Weather/Special duties/Incidents:

_____

_____

_____

_____

_____

Certifying Signature:
Captain or Owners Signature   _____

Captain's Log ASA Documented Sailing Time

Dates   Leave: Arrive:

Times   Leave: Arrive:

Location   Origin:

                     Destination:

VesselName: LOA:

Type: Size: Tonnage:

Number of Days on Board:

Distance logged:

Night hours/watch:

Details of voyage:

                     Crew/Position/Weather/Special duties/Incidents:

_____

_____

_____

_____

Certifying Signature:
Captain or Owners Signature   _____

Captain's Log ASA Documented Sailing Time

Dates　　　Leave:　　　　　　　　Arrive:

Times　　　Leave:　　　　　　　　Arrive:

Location　　　Origin:

　　　　　　　Destination:

VesselName:　　　　　　　　LOA:

Type:　　　　　　　Size:　　　　　　　Tonnage:

Number of Days on Board:

Distance logged:

Night hours/watch:

Details of voyage:

Crew/Position/Weather/Special duties/Incidents:

_____

_____

_____

_____

_____

Certifying Signature:
Captain or Owners Signature　_____

Captain's Log ASA Documented Sailing Time

Dates   Leave: Arrive:

Times   Leave: Arrive:

Location   Origin:

                 Destination:

VesselName: LOA:

Type: Size: Tonnage:

Number of Days on Board:

Distance logged:

Night hours/watch:

Details of voyage:

                 Crew/Position/Weather/Special duties/Incidents:

_____

_____

_____

_____

Certifying Signature:
Captain or Owners Signature   _____

Captain's Log ASA Documented Sailing Time

Dates   Leave: Arrive:

Times   Leave: Arrive:

Location   Origin:

Destination:

VesselName: LOA:

Type: Size: Tonnage:

Number of Days on Board:

Distance logged:

Night hours/watch:

Details of voyage:

Crew/Position/Weather/Special duties/Incidents:

_____

_____

_____

_____

Certifying Signature:
Captain or Owners Signature _____

Captain's Log ASA Documented Sailing Time

Dates   Leave: Arrive:

Times   Leave: Arrive:

Location   Origin:

                Destination:

VesselName: LOA:

Type: Size: Tonnage:

Number of Days on Board:

Distance logged:

Night hours/watch:

Details of voyage:

Crew/Position/Weather/Special duties/Incidents:

_____

_____

_____

_____

Certifying Signature:
Captain or Owners Signature   _____

Captain's Log ASA Documented Sailing Time

Dates   Leave: Arrive:

Times   Leave: Arrive:

Location   Origin:

                        Destination:

VesselName: LOA:

Type: Size: Tonnage:

Number of Days on Board:

Distance logged:

Night hours/watch:

Details of voyage:

Crew/Position/Weather/Special duties/Incidents:

_____

_____

_____

_____

_____

Certifying Signature:
Captain or Owners Signature   _____

Captain's Log ASA Documented Sailing Time

Dates   Leave: Arrive:

Times   Leave: Arrive:

Location   Origin:

                   Destination:

VesselName: LOA:

Type: Size: Tonnage:

Number of Days on Board:

Distance logged:

Night hours/watch:

Details of voyage:

             Crew/Position/Weather/Special duties/Incidents:

_____

_____

_____

_____

Certifying Signature:
Captain or Owners Signature   _____

Captain's Log ASA Documented Sailing Time

Dates   Leave: Arrive:

Times   Leave: Arrive:

Location   Origin:

           Destination:

VesselName: LOA:

Type: Size: Tonnage:

Number of Days on Board:

Distance logged:

Night hours/watch:

Details of voyage:

           Crew/Position/Weather/Special duties/Incidents:

_____

_____

_____

_____

Certifying Signature:
Captain or Owners Signature   _____

Captain's Log ASA Documented Sailing Time

Dates   Leave: Arrive:

Times   Leave: Arrive:

Location   Origin:

                     Destination:

VesselName: LOA:

Type: Size: Tonnage:

Number of Days on Board:

Distance logged:

Night hours/watch:

Details of voyage:

                    Crew/Position/Weather/Special duties/Incidents:

_____

_____

_____

_____

_____

Certifying Signature:
Captain or Owners Signature   _____

Captain's Log ASA Documented Sailing Time

Dates   Leave: Arrive:

Times   Leave: Arrive:

Location   Origin:

Destination:

VesselName: LOA:

Type: Size: Tonnage:

Number of Days on Board:

Distance logged:

Night hours/watch:

Details of voyage:

Crew/Position/Weather/Special duties/Incidents:

_____

_____

_____

_____

Certifying Signature:
Captain or Owners Signature   _____

Captain's Log ASA Documented Sailing Time

Dates   Leave: Arrive:

Times   Leave: Arrive:

Location   Origin:

                    Destination:

VesselName: LOA:

Type: Size: Tonnage:

Number of Days on Board:

Distance logged:

Night hours/watch:

Details of voyage:

Crew/Position/Weather/Special duties/Incidents:

_____

_____

_____

_____

Certifying Signature:
Captain or Owners Signature   _____

Captain's Log ASA Documented Sailing Time

__Dates__   Leave: Arrive:

__Times__   Leave: Arrive:

__Location__   Origin:

                Destination:

__VesselName:__   LOA:

Type: Size: Tonnage:

__Number of Days on Board:__

__Distance logged:__

__Night hours/watch:__

__Details of voyage:__

                Crew/Position/Weather/Special duties/Incidents:

_____

_____

_____

_____

__Certifying Signature:__

Captain or Owners Signature   _____

Captain's Log ASA Documented Sailing Time

Dates   Leave: Arrive:

Times   Leave: Arrive:

Location   Origin:

                          Destination:

VesselName: LOA:

Type: Size: Tonnage:

Number of Days on Board:

Distance logged:

Night hours/watch:

Details of voyage:

                    Crew/Position/Weather/Special duties/Incidents:

_____

_____

_____

_____

_____

Certifying Signature:
Captain or Owners Signature   _____

Captain's Log ASA Documented Sailing Time

Dates   Leave: Arrive:

Times   Leave: Arrive:

Location   Origin:

                Destination:

VesselName: LOA:

Type: Size: Tonnage:

Number of Days on Board:

Distance logged:

Night hours/watch:

Details of voyage:

Crew/Position/Weather/Special duties/Incidents:

_____

_____

_____

_____

Certifying Signature:
Captain or Owners Signature _____

Captain's Log ASA Documented Sailing Time

Dates   Leave: Arrive:

Times   Leave: Arrive:

Location   Origin:

Destination:

VesselName: LOA:

Type: Size: Tonnage:

Number of Days on Board:

Distance logged:

Night hours/watch:

Details of voyage:

Crew/Position/Weather/Special duties/Incidents:

_____

_____

_____

_____

Certifying Signature:
Captain or Owners Signature _____

Captain's Log ASA Documented Sailing Time

Dates   Leave: Arrive:

Times   Leave: Arrive:

Location   Origin:

                   Destination:

VesselName: LOA:

Type: Size: Tonnage:

Number of Days on Board:

Distance logged:

Night hours/watch:

Details of voyage:

Crew/Position/Weather/Special duties/Incidents:

_____

_____

_____

_____

_____

Certifying Signature:
Captain or Owners Signature _____

Captain's Log ASA Documented Sailing Time

Dates   Leave: Arrive:

Times   Leave: Arrive:

Location   Origin:

Destination:

VesselName: LOA:

Type: Size: Tonnage:

Number of Days on Board:

Distance logged:

Night hours/watch:

Details of voyage:

Crew/Position/Weather/Special duties/Incidents:

_____

_____

_____

_____

Certifying Signature:
Captain or Owners Signature   _____

Captain's Log ASA Documented Sailing Time

Dates   Leave: Arrive:

Times   Leave: Arrive:

Location   Origin:

                   Destination:

Vessel Name: LOA:

Type: Size: Tonnage:

Number of Days on Board:

Distance logged:

Night hours/watch:

Details of voyage:

            Crew/Position/Weather/Special duties/Incidents:

_____

_____

_____

_____

_____

Certifying Signature:
Captain or Owners Signature _____

Captain's Log ASA Documented Sailing Time

Dates   Leave: Arrive:

Times   Leave: Arrive:

Location   Origin:

                     Destination:

VesselName: LOA:

Type: Size: Tonnage:

Number of Days on Board:

Distance logged:

Night hours/watch:

Details of voyage:

Crew/Position/Weather/Special duties/Incidents:

_____

_____

_____

_____

Certifying Signature:
Captain or Owners Signature _____

Captain's Log ASA Documented Sailing Time

Dates   Leave: Arrive:

Times   Leave: Arrive:

Location   Origin:

                   Destination:

VesselName: LOA:

Type: Size: Tonnage:

Number of Days on Board:

Distance logged:

Night hours/watch:

Details of voyage:

Crew/Position/Weather/Special duties/Incidents:

_____

_____

_____

_____

Certifying Signature:
Captain or Owners Signature _____

Captain's Log ASA Documented Sailing Time

Dates   Leave: Arrive:

Times   Leave: Arrive:

Location   Origin:

                   Destination:

VesselName: LOA:

Type: Size: Tonnage:

Number of Days on Board:

Distance logged:

Night hours/watch:

Details of voyage:

Crew/Position/Weather/Special duties/Incidents:

_____

_____

_____

_____

Certifying Signature:
Captain or Owners Signature _____

Captain's Log ASA Documented Sailing Time

Dates   Leave: Arrive:

Times   Leave: Arrive:

Location   Origin:

          Destination:

Vessel Name: LOA:

Type: Size: Tonnage:

Number of Days on Board:

Distance logged:

Night hours/watch:

Details of voyage:

          Crew/Position/Weather/Special duties/Incidents:

_____

_____

_____

_____

Certifying Signature:
Captain or Owners Signature   _____

Captain's Log ASA Documented Sailing Time

Dates   Leave: Arrive:

Times   Leave: Arrive:

Location   Origin:

               Destination:

VesselName: LOA:

Type: Size: Tonnage:

Number of Days on Board:

Distance logged:

Night hours/watch:

Details of voyage:

                    Crew/Position/Weather/Special duties/Incidents:

_____

_____

_____

_____

Certifying Signature:
Captain or Owners Signature   _____

Captain's Log ASA Documented Sailing Time

Dates   Leave: Arrive:

Times   Leave: Arrive:

Location   Origin:

                        Destination:

VesselName: LOA:

Type: Size: Tonnage:

Number of Days on Board:

Distance logged:

Night hours/watch:

Details of voyage:

Crew/Position/Weather/Special duties/Incidents:

_____

_____

_____

_____

Certifying Signature:
Captain or Owners Signature _____

Captain's Log ASA Documented Sailing Time

Dates   Leave: Arrive:

Times   Leave: Arrive:

Location   Origin:

                     Destination:

VesselName: LOA:

Type: Size: Tonnage:

Number of Days on Board:

Distance logged:

Night hours/watch:

Details of voyage:

Crew/Position/Weather/Special duties/Incidents:

_____

_____

_____

_____

_____

Certifying Signature:

Captain or Owners Signature   _____

Captain's Log ASA Documented Sailing Time

Dates   Leave: Arrive:

Times   Leave: Arrive:

Location   Origin:

                  Destination:

VesselName: LOA:

Type: Size: Tonnage:

Number of Days on Board:

Distance logged:

Night hours/watch:

Details of voyage:

Crew/Position/Weather/Special duties/Incidents:

_____

_____

_____

_____

Certifying Signature:
Captain or Owners Signature   _____

Captain's Log ASA Documented Sailing Time

Dates   Leave: Arrive:

Times   Leave: Arrive:

Location   Origin:

                Destination:

VesselName: LOA:

Type: Size: Tonnage:

Number of Days on Board:

Distance logged:

Night hours/watch:

Details of voyage:

Crew/Position/Weather/Special duties/Incidents:

_____

_____

_____

_____

_____

Certifying Signature:
Captain or Owners Signature   _____

Captain's Log ASA Documented Sailing Time

Dates   Leave: Arrive:

Times   Leave: Arrive:

Location   Origin:

                    Destination:

VesselName: LOA:

Type: Size: Tonnage:

Number of Days on Board:

Distance logged:

Night hours/watch:

Details of voyage:

Crew/Position/Weather/Special duties/Incidents:

_____

_____

_____

_____

Certifying Signature:
Captain or Owners Signature   _____

Captain's Log ASA Documented Sailing Time

Dates   Leave: Arrive:

Times   Leave: Arrive:

Location   Origin:

                         Destination:

VesselName: LOA:

Type: Size: Tonnage:

Number of Days on Board:

Distance logged:

Night hours/watch:

Details of voyage:

Crew/Position/Weather/Special duties/Incidents:

_____

_____

_____

_____

_____

Certifying Signature:
Captain or Owners Signature _____

Captain's Log ASA Documented Sailing Time

Dates   Leave: Arrive:

Times   Leave: Arrive:

Location   Origin:

               Destination:

VesselName: LOA:

Type: Size: Tonnage:

Number of Days on Board:

Distance logged:

Night hours/watch:

Details of voyage:

Crew/Position/Weather/Special duties/Incidents:

_____

_____

_____

_____

Certifying Signature:
Captain or Owners Signature   _____

Captain's Log ASA Documented Sailing Time

Dates   Leave: Arrive:

Times   Leave: Arrive:

Location   Origin:

                     Destination:

VesselName: LOA:

Type: Size: Tonnage:

Number of Days on Board:

Distance logged:

Night hours/watch:

Details of voyage:

Crew/Position/Weather/Special duties/Incidents:

_____

_____

_____

_____

Certifying Signature:
Captain or Owners Signature   _____

Captain's Log ASA Documented Sailing Time

Dates   Leave: Arrive:

Times   Leave: Arrive:

Location   Origin:

Destination:

VesselName: LOA:

Type: Size: Tonnage:

Number of Days on Board:

Distance logged:

Night hours/watch:

Details of voyage:

Crew/Position/Weather/Special duties/Incidents:

_____

_____

_____

_____

Certifying Signature:
Captain or Owners Signature _____

Captain's Log ASA Documented Sailing Time

Dates   Leave: Arrive:

Times   Leave: Arrive:

Location   Origin:

                   Destination:

VesselName: LOA:

Type: Size: Tonnage:

Number of Days on Board:

Distance logged:

Night hours/watch:

Details of voyage:

Crew/Position/Weather/Special duties/Incidents:

_____

_____

_____

_____

Certifying Signature:
Captain or Owners Signature _____

Captain's Log ASA Documented Sailing Time

Dates   Leave: Arrive:

Times   Leave: Arrive:

Location   Origin:

                Destination:

VesselName: LOA:

Type: Size: Tonnage:

Number of Days on Board:

Distance logged:

Night hours/watch:

Details of voyage:

Crew/Position/Weather/Special duties/Incidents:

_____

_____

_____

_____

Certifying Signature:
Captain or Owners Signature _____

Captain's Log ASA Documented Sailing Time

Dates   Leave: Arrive:

Times   Leave: Arrive:

Location   Origin:

                    Destination:

VesselName: LOA:

Type: Size: Tonnage:

Number of Days on Board:

Distance logged:

Night hours/watch:

Details of voyage:

                    Crew/Position/Weather/Special duties/Incidents:

_____

_____

_____

_____

Certifying Signature:
Captain or Owners Signature   _____

Captain's Log ASA Documented Sailing Time

Dates   Leave: Arrive:

Times   Leave: Arrive:

Location   Origin:

                     Destination:

VesselName: LOA:

Type: Size: Tonnage:

Number of Days on Board:

Distance logged:

Night hours/watch:

Details of voyage:

Crew/Position/Weather/Special duties/Incidents:

_____

_____

_____

_____

Certifying Signature:
Captain or Owners Signature _____

Captain's Log ASA Documented Sailing Time

Dates   Leave: Arrive:

Times   Leave: Arrive:

Location   Origin:

                   Destination:

VesselName: LOA:

Type: Size: Tonnage:

Number of Days on Board:

Distance logged:

Night hours/watch:

Details of voyage:

                   Crew/Position/Weather/Special duties/Incidents:

_____

_____

_____

_____

Certifying Signature:
Captain or Owners Signature   _____

Captain's Log ASA Documented Sailing Time

Dates   Leave: Arrive:

Times   Leave: Arrive:

Location   Origin:

Destination:

VesselName: LOA:

Type: Size: Tonnage:

Number of Days on Board:

Distance logged:

Night hours/watch:

Details of voyage:

Crew/Position/Weather/Special duties/Incidents:

_____

_____

_____

_____

_____

Certifying Signature:
Captain or Owners Signature   _____

Captain's Log ASA Documented Sailing Time

Dates   Leave: Arrive:

Times   Leave: Arrive:

Location   Origin:

                        Destination:

VesselName: LOA:

Type: Size: Tonnage:

Number of Days on Board:

Distance logged:

Night hours/watch:

Details of voyage:

             Crew/Position/Weather/Special duties/Incidents:

_____

_____

_____

_____

_____

Certifying Signature:
Captain or Owners Signature _____

Captain's Log ASA Documented Sailing Time

Dates   Leave: Arrive:

Times   Leave: Arrive:

Location   Origin:

                   Destination:

VesselName: LOA:

Type: Size: Tonnage:

Number of Days on Board:

Distance logged:

Night hours/watch:

Details of voyage:

Crew/Position/Weather/Special duties/Incidents:

_____

_____

_____

_____

Certifying Signature:
Captain or Owners Signature _____

Captain's Log ASA Documented Sailing Time

Dates   Leave: Arrive:

Times   Leave: Arrive:

Location   Origin:

                   Destination:

VesselName: LOA:

Type: Size: Tonnage:

Number of Days on Board:

Distance logged:

Night hours/watch:

Details of voyage:

Crew/Position/Weather/Special duties/Incidents:

_____

_____

_____

_____

_____

Certifying Signature:

Captain or Owners Signature _____

Captain's Log ASA Documented Sailing Time

Dates   Leave: Arrive:

Times   Leave: Arrive:

Location   Origin:

                   Destination:

VesselName: LOA:

Type: Size: Tonnage:

Number of Days on Board:

Distance logged:

Night hours/watch:

Details of voyage:

                   Crew/Position/Weather/Special duties/Incidents:

_____

_____

_____

_____

Certifying Signature:
Captain or Owners Signature   _____

Captain's Log ASA Documented Sailing Time

Dates   Leave: Arrive:

Times   Leave: Arrive:

Location   Origin:

                   Destination:

VesselName: LOA:

Type: Size: Tonnage:

Number of Days on Board:

Distance logged:

Night hours/watch:

Details of voyage:

Crew/Position/Weather/Special duties/Incidents:

_____

_____

_____

_____

Certifying Signature:
Captain or Owners Signature   _____

Captain's Log ASA Documented Sailing Time

Dates   Leave: Arrive:

Times   Leave: Arrive:

Location   Origin:

                   Destination:

VesselName: LOA:

Type: Size: Tonnage:

Number of Days on Board:

Distance logged:

Night hours/watch:

Details of voyage:

Crew/Position/Weather/Special duties/Incidents:

_____

_____

_____

_____

Certifying Signature:
Captain or Owners Signature _____

Captain's Log ASA Documented Sailing Time

Dates   Leave: Arrive:

Times   Leave: Arrive:

Location   Origin:

                   Destination:

VesselName: LOA:

Type: Size: Tonnage:

Number of Days on Board:

Distance logged:

Night hours/watch:

Details of voyage:

Crew/Position/Weather/Special duties/Incidents:

_____

_____

_____

_____

Certifying Signature:
Captain or Owners Signature   _____

Captain's Log ASA Documented Sailing Time

Dates   Leave: Arrive:

Times   Leave: Arrive:

Location   Origin:

                   Destination:

VesselName: LOA:

Type: Size: Tonnage:

Number of Days on Board:

Distance logged:

Night hours/watch:

Details of voyage:

        Crew/Position/Weather/Special duties/Incidents:

_____

_____

_____

_____

Certifying Signature:
Captain or Owners Signature   _____

Captain's Log ASA Documented Sailing Time

Dates   Leave: Arrive:

Times   Leave: Arrive:

Location   Origin:

                    Destination:

VesselName: LOA:

Type: Size: Tonnage:

Number of Days on Board:

Distance logged:

Night hours/watch:

Details of voyage:

                    Crew/Position/Weather/Special duties/Incidents:

_____

_____

_____

_____

Certifying Signature:
Captain or Owners Signature   _____

Captain's Log ASA Documented Sailing Time

Dates   Leave: Arrive:

Times   Leave: Arrive:

Location   Origin:

                   Destination:

VesselName: LOA:

Type: Size: Tonnage:

Number of Days on Board:

Distance logged:

Night hours/watch:

Details of voyage:

                   Crew/Position/Weather/Special duties/Incidents:

_____

_____

_____

_____

_____

Certifying Signature:
Captain or Owners Signature   _____

Captain's Log ASA Documented Sailing Time

Dates   Leave: Arrive:

Times   Leave: Arrive:

Location   Origin:

Destination:

VesselName: LOA:

Type: Size: Tonnage:

Number of Days on Board:

Distance logged:

Night hours/watch:

Details of voyage:

Crew/Position/Weather/Special duties/Incidents:

_____

_____

_____

_____

_____

Certifying Signature:
Captain or Owners Signature   _____

Captain's Log ASA Documented Sailing Time

Dates   Leave: Arrive:

Times   Leave: Arrive:

Location   Origin:

                Destination:

VesselName: LOA:

Type: Size: Tonnage:

Number of Days on Board:

Distance logged:

Night hours/watch:

Details of voyage:

                Crew/Position/Weather/Special duties/Incidents:

_____

_____

_____

_____

Certifying Signature:
Captain or Owners Signature   _____

Captain's Log ASA Documented Sailing Time

Dates   Leave: Arrive:

Times   Leave: Arrive:

Location   Origin:

                   Destination:

VesselName: LOA:

Type: Size: Tonnage:

Number of Days on Board:

Distance logged:

Night hours/watch:

Details of voyage:

Crew/Position/Weather/Special duties/Incidents:

_____

_____

_____

_____

Certifying Signature:
Captain or Owners Signature   _____

Captain's Log ASA Documented Sailing Time

Dates   Leave: Arrive:

Times   Leave: Arrive:

Location   Origin:

                    Destination:

Vessel Name: LOA:

Type: Size: Tonnage:

Number of Days on Board:

Distance logged:

Night hours/watch:

Details of voyage:

Crew/Position/Weather/Special duties/Incidents:

_____

_____

_____

_____

Certifying Signature:
Captain or Owners Signature _____

Captain's Log ASA Documented Sailing Time

Dates   Leave: Arrive:

Times   Leave: Arrive:

Location   Origin:

                              Destination:

VesselName: LOA:

Type: Size: Tonnage:

Number of Days on Board:

Distance logged:

Night hours/watch:

Details of voyage:

          Crew/Position/Weather/Special duties/Incidents:

_____

_____

_____

_____

Certifying Signature:
Captain or Owners Signature   _____

Captain's Log ASA Documented Sailing Time

Dates   Leave: Arrive:

Times   Leave: Arrive:

Location   Origin:

                     Destination:

Vessel Name: LOA:

Type: Size: Tonnage:

Number of Days on Board:

Distance logged:

Night hours/watch:

Details of voyage:

Crew/Position/Weather/Special duties/Incidents:

_____

_____

_____

_____

Certifying Signature:

Captain or Owners Signature   _____

Captain's Log ASA Documented Sailing Time

Dates   Leave: Arrive:

Times   Leave: Arrive:

Location   Origin:

                  Destination:

Vessel Name: LOA:

Type: Size: Tonnage:

Number of Days on Board:

Distance logged:

Night hours/watch:

Details of voyage:

Crew/Position/Weather/Special duties/Incidents:

_____

_____

_____

_____

Certifying Signature:
Captain or Owners Signature _____

Captain's Log ASA Documented Sailing Time

Dates   Leave: Arrive:

Times   Leave: Arrive:

Location   Origin:

                 Destination:

Vessel Name: LOA:

Type: Size: Tonnage:

Number of Days on Board:

Distance logged:

Night hours/watch:

Details of voyage:

Crew/Position/Weather/Special duties/Incidents:

_____

_____

_____

_____

Certifying Signature:
Captain or Owners Signature   _____

Captain's Log ASA Documented Sailing Time

Dates   Leave: Arrive:

Times   Leave: Arrive:

Location   Origin:

                   Destination:

VesselName: LOA:

Type: Size: Tonnage:

Number of Days on Board:

Distance logged:

Night hours/watch:

Details of voyage:

Crew/Position/Weather/Special duties/Incidents:

_____

_____

_____

_____

_____

Certifying Signature:
Captain or Owners Signature   _____

Captain's Log ASA Documented Sailing Time

Dates   Leave: Arrive:

Times   Leave: Arrive:

Location   Origin:

                 Destination:

VesselName: LOA:

Type: Size: Tonnage:

Number of Days on Board:

Distance logged:

Night hours/watch:

Details of voyage:

                 Crew/Position/Weather/Special duties/Incidents:

_____

_____

_____

_____

Certifying Signature:
Captain or Owners Signature   _____

Captain's Log ASA Documented Sailing Time

Dates   Leave: Arrive:

Times   Leave: Arrive:

Location   Origin:

                Destination:

VesselName: LOA:

Type: Size: Tonnage:

Number of Days on Board:

Distance logged:

Night hours/watch:

Details of voyage:

Crew/Position/Weather/Special duties/Incidents:

_____

_____

_____

_____

Certifying Signature:
Captain or Owners Signature   _____

Captain's Log ASA Documented Sailing Time

Dates   Leave: Arrive:

Times   Leave: Arrive:

Location   Origin:

                    Destination:

VesselName: LOA:

Type: Size: Tonnage:

Number of Days on Board:

Distance logged:

Night hours/watch:

Details of voyage:

          Crew/Position/Weather/Special duties/Incidents:

_____

_____

_____

_____

Certifying Signature:
Captain or Owners Signature _____

Captain's Log ASA Documented Sailing Time

Dates   Leave: Arrive:

Times   Leave: Arrive:

Location   Origin:

                 Destination:

VesselName: LOA:

Type: Size: Tonnage:

Number of Days on Board:

Distance logged:

Night hours/watch:

Details of voyage:

Crew/Position/Weather/Special duties/Incidents:

_____

_____

_____

_____

Certifying Signature:
Captain or Owners Signature _____

Captain's Log ASA Documented Sailing Time

Dates   Leave: Arrive:

Times   Leave: Arrive:

Location   Origin:

                    Destination:

VesselName: LOA:

Type: Size: Tonnage:

Number of Days on Board:

Distance logged:

Night hours/watch:

Details of voyage:

Crew/Position/Weather/Special duties/Incidents:

_____

_____

_____

_____

Certifying Signature:
Captain or Owners Signature   _____

Captain's Log ASA Documented Sailing Time

Dates   Leave: Arrive:

Times   Leave: Arrive:

Location   Origin:

                 Destination:

VesselName: LOA:

Type: Size: Tonnage:

Number of Days on Board:

Distance logged:

Night hours/watch:

Details of voyage:

                 Crew/Position/Weather/Special duties/Incidents:

_____

_____

_____

_____

Certifying Signature:
Captain or Owners Signature _____

Captain's Log ASA Documented Sailing Time

Dates   Leave: Arrive:

Times   Leave: Arrive:

Location   Origin:

                  Destination:

VesselName: LOA:

Type: Size: Tonnage:

Number of Days on Board:

Distance logged:

Night hours/watch:

Details of voyage:

         Crew/Position/Weather/Special duties/Incidents:

_____

_____

_____

_____

Certifying Signature:
Captain or Owners Signature   _____

Captain's Log ASA Documented Sailing Time

Dates   Leave: Arrive:

Times   Leave: Arrive:

Location   Origin:

                   Destination:

VesselName: LOA:

Type: Size: Tonnage:

Number of Days on Board:

Distance logged:

Night hours/watch:

Details of voyage:

Crew/Position/Weather/Special duties/Incidents:

_____

_____

_____

_____

Certifying Signature:
Captain or Owners Signature   _____

Captain's Log ASA Documented Sailing Time

Dates   Leave: Arrive:

Times   Leave: Arrive:

Location   Origin:

                        Destination:

VesselName: LOA:

Type: Size: Tonnage:

Number of Days on Board:

Distance logged:

Night hours/watch:

Details of voyage:

Crew/Position/Weather/Special duties/Incidents:

_____

_____

_____

_____

_____

Certifying Signature:
Captain or Owners Signature _____

Captain's Log ASA Documented Sailing Time

Dates   Leave: _____   Arrive: _____

Times   Leave: _____   Arrive: _____

Location   Origin: _____

Destination: _____

VesselName: _____   LOA: _____

Type: _____   Size: _____   Tonnage: _____

Number of Days on Board: _____

Distance logged: _____

Night hours/watch: _____

Details of voyage: _____

Crew/Position/Weather/Special duties/Incidents:

_____

_____

_____

_____

Certifying Signature:
Captain or Owners Signature   _____

Captain's Log ASA Documented Sailing Time

Dates   Leave: Arrive:

Times   Leave: Arrive:

Location   Origin:

                    Destination:

VesselName: LOA:

Type: Size: Tonnage:

Number of Days on Board:

Distance logged:

Night hours/watch:

Details of voyage:

                    Crew/Position/Weather/Special duties/Incidents:

_____

_____

_____

_____

Certifying Signature:
Captain or Owners Signature _____

Captain's Log ASA Documented Sailing Time

Dates   Leave: Arrive:

Times   Leave: Arrive:

Location   Origin:

                Destination:

VesselName: LOA:

Type: Size: Tonnage:

Number of Days on Board:

Distance logged:

Night hours/watch:

Details of voyage:

Crew/Position/Weather/Special duties/Incidents:

_____

_____

_____

_____

Certifying Signature:
Captain or Owners Signature _____

Captain's Log ASA Documented Sailing Time

Dates   Leave: Arrive:

Times   Leave: Arrive:

Location   Origin:

                   Destination:

VesselName: LOA:

Type: Size: Tonnage:

Number of Days on Board:

Distance logged:

Night hours/watch:

Details of voyage:

Crew/Position/Weather/Special duties/Incidents:

_____

_____

_____

_____

Certifying Signature:
Captain or Owners Signature   _____

Captain's Log ASA Documented Sailing Time

Dates   Leave: Arrive:

Times   Leave: Arrive:

Location   Origin:

                   Destination:

VesselName: LOA:

Type: Size: Tonnage:

Number of Days on Board:

Distance logged:

Night hours/watch:

Details of voyage:

                   Crew/Position/Weather/Special duties/Incidents:

_____

_____

_____

_____

Certifying Signature:
Captain or Owners Signature   _____

Captain's Log ASA Documented Sailing Time

Dates   Leave: Arrive:

Times   Leave: Arrive:

Location   Origin:

                    Destination:

VesselName: LOA:

Type: Size: Tonnage:

Number of Days on Board:

Distance logged:

Night hours/watch:

Details of voyage:

Crew/Position/Weather/Special duties/Incidents:

_____

_____

_____

_____

Certifying Signature:
Captain or Owners Signature   _____

Captain's Log ASA Documented Sailing Time

Dates   Leave: Arrive:

Times   Leave: Arrive:

Location   Origin:

                    Destination:

VesselName: LOA:

Type: Size: Tonnage:

Number of Days on Board:

Distance logged:

Night hours/watch:

Details of voyage:

Crew/Position/Weather/Special duties/Incidents:

_____

_____

_____

_____

_____

Certifying Signature:
Captain or Owners Signature _____

Captain's Log ASA Documented Sailing Time

Dates   Leave: Arrive:

Times   Leave: Arrive:

Location   Origin:

Destination:

VesselName: LOA:

Type: Size: Tonnage:

Number of Days on Board:

Distance logged:

Night hours/watch:

Details of voyage:

Crew/Position/Weather/Special duties/Incidents:

_____

_____

_____

_____

Certifying Signature:
Captain or Owners Signature   _____

Captain's Log ASA Documented Sailing Time

Dates   Leave: Arrive:

Times   Leave: Arrive:

Location   Origin:

                   Destination:

VesselName: LOA:

Type: Size: Tonnage:

Number of Days on Board:

Distance logged:

Night hours/watch:

Details of voyage:

Crew/Position/Weather/Special duties/Incidents:

_____

_____

_____

_____

Certifying Signature:
Captain or Owners Signature _____

Captain's Log ASA Documented Sailing Time

Dates   Leave: Arrive:

Times   Leave: Arrive:

Location   Origin:

                    Destination:

VesselName: LOA:

Type: Size: Tonnage:

Number of Days on Board:

Distance logged:

Night hours/watch:

Details of voyage:

Crew/Position/Weather/Special duties/Incidents:

_____

_____

_____

_____

Certifying Signature:
Captain or Owners Signature _____

Captain's Log ASA Documented Sailing Time

Dates   Leave: Arrive:

Times   Leave: Arrive:

Location   Origin:

                        Destination:

VesselName: LOA:

Type: Size: Tonnage:

Number of Days on Board:

Distance logged:

Night hours/watch:

Details of voyage:

                Crew/Position/Weather/Special duties/Incidents:

_____

_____

_____

_____

Certifying Signature:
Captain or Owners Signature _____

Captain's Log ASA Documented Sailing Time

Dates Leave: Arrive:

Times Leave: Arrive:

Location Origin:

Destination:

VesselName: LOA:

Type: Size: Tonnage:

Number of Days on Board:

Distance logged:

Night hours/watch:

Details of voyage:

Crew/Position/Weather/Special duties/Incidents:

_____

_____

_____

_____

Certifying Signature:
Captain or Owners Signature   _____

Captain's Log ASA Documented Sailing Time

Dates   Leave: Arrive:

Times   Leave: Arrive:

Location   Origin:

                   Destination:

VesselName: LOA:

Type: Size: Tonnage:

Number of Days on Board:

Distance logged:

Night hours/watch:

Details of voyage:

Crew/Position/Weather/Special duties/Incidents:

_____

_____

_____

_____

_____

Certifying Signature:
Captain or Owners Signature _____

Captain's Log ASA Documented Sailing Time

Dates   Leave: Arrive:

Times   Leave: Arrive:

Location   Origin:

                   Destination:

VesselName: LOA:

Type: Size: Tonnage:

Number of Days on Board:

Distance logged:

Night hours/watch:

Details of voyage:

Crew/Position/Weather/Special duties/Incidents:

_____

_____

_____

_____

Certifying Signature:

Captain or Owners Signature   _____

Captain's Log ASA Documented Sailing Time

Dates   Leave: Arrive:

Times   Leave: Arrive:

Location   Origin:

Destination:

Vessel Name: LOA:

Type: Size: Tonnage:

Number of Days on Board:

Distance logged:

Night hours/watch:

Details of voyage:

Crew/Position/Weather/Special duties/Incidents:

_____

_____

_____

_____

Certifying Signature:
Captain or Owners Signature   _____

Captain's Log ASA Documented Sailing Time

Dates   Leave: Arrive:

Times   Leave: Arrive:

Location   Origin:

Destination:

VesselName: LOA:

Type: Size: Tonnage:

Number of Days on Board:

Distance logged:

Night hours/watch:

Details of voyage:

Crew/Position/Weather/Special duties/Incidents:

_____

_____

_____

_____

Certifying Signature:
Captain or Owners Signature   _____

Captain's Log ASA Documented Sailing Time

Dates   Leave: Arrive:

Times   Leave: Arrive:

Location   Origin:

                    Destination:

VesselName: LOA:

Type: Size: Tonnage:

Number of Days on Board:

Distance logged:

Night hours/watch:

Details of voyage:

                    Crew/Position/Weather/Special duties/Incidents:

_____

_____

_____

_____

Certifying Signature:
Captain or Owners Signature   _____

Captain's Log ASA Documented Sailing Time

Dates   Leave: Arrive:

Times   Leave: Arrive:

Location   Origin:

                     Destination:

VesselName: LOA:

Type: Size: Tonnage:

Number of Days on Board:

Distance logged:

Night hours/watch:

Details of voyage:

Crew/Position/Weather/Special duties/Incidents:

_____

_____

_____

_____

Certifying Signature:
Captain or Owners Signature   _____

Captain's Log ASA Documented Sailing Time

Dates   Leave: Arrive:

Times   Leave: Arrive:

Location   Origin:

                     Destination:

VesselName: LOA:

Type: Size: Tonnage:

Number of Days on Board:

Distance logged:

Night hours/watch:

Details of voyage:

                 Crew/Position/Weather/Special duties/Incidents:

_____

_____

_____

_____

Certifying Signature:
Captain or Owners Signature   _____

Captain's Log ASA Documented Sailing Time

Dates   Leave: Arrive:

Times   Leave: Arrive:

Location   Origin:

                    Destination:

VesselName: LOA:

Type: Size: Tonnage:

Number of Days on Board:

Distance logged:

Night hours/watch:

Details of voyage:

Crew/Position/Weather/Special duties/Incidents:

_____

_____

_____

_____

Certifying Signature:
Captain or Owners Signature   _____

Captain's Log ASA Documented Sailing Time

Dates   Leave: Arrive:

Times   Leave: Arrive:

Location   Origin:

                    Destination:

VesselName: LOA:

Type: Size: Tonnage:

Number of Days on Board:

Distance logged:

Night hours/watch:

Details of voyage:

Crew/Position/Weather/Special duties/Incidents:

_____

_____

_____

_____

Certifying Signature:
Captain or Owners Signature   _____

Captain's Log ASA Documented Sailing Time

Dates   Leave: Arrive:

Times   Leave: Arrive:

Location   Origin:

                 Destination:

Vessel Name: LOA:

Type: Size: Tonnage:

Number of Days on Board:

Distance logged:

Night hours/watch:

Details of voyage:

        Crew/Position/Weather/Special duties/Incidents:

_____

_____

_____

_____

Certifying Signature:
Captain or Owners Signature   _____

Captain's Log ASA Documented Sailing Time

Dates   Leave: Arrive:

Times   Leave: Arrive:

Location   Origin:

                   Destination:

VesselName: LOA:

Type: Size: Tonnage:

Number of Days on Board:

Distance logged:

Night hours/watch:

Details of voyage:

                   Crew/Position/Weather/Special duties/Incidents:

_____

_____

_____

_____

_____

Certifying Signature:

Captain or Owners Signature _____

Captain's Log ASA Documented Sailing Time

Dates   Leave: Arrive:

Times   Leave: Arrive:

Location   Origin:

                    Destination:

VesselName: LOA:

Type: Size: Tonnage:

Number of Days on Board:

Distance logged:

Night hours/watch:

Details of voyage:

Crew/Position/Weather/Special duties/Incidents:

_____

_____

_____

_____

Certifying Signature:
Captain or Owners Signature   _____

Captain's Log ASA Documented Sailing Time

Dates   Leave: Arrive:

Times   Leave: Arrive:

Location   Origin:

                Destination:

VesselName: LOA:

Type: Size: Tonnage:

Number of Days on Board:

Distance logged:

Night hours/watch:

Details of voyage:

Crew/Position/Weather/Special duties/Incidents:

_____

_____

_____

_____

_____

Certifying Signature:
Captain or Owners Signature _____

Captain's Log ASA Documented Sailing Time

Dates   Leave: Arrive:

Times   Leave: Arrive:

Location   Origin:

                     Destination:

VesselName: LOA:

Type: Size: Tonnage:

Number of Days on Board:

Distance logged:

Night hours/watch:

Details of voyage:

Crew/Position/Weather/Special duties/Incidents:

_____

_____

_____

_____

Certifying Signature:
Captain or Owners Signature _____

Captain's Log ASA Documented Sailing Time

Dates   Leave: Arrive:

Times   Leave: Arrive:

Location   Origin:

                 Destination:

VesselName: LOA:

Type: Size: Tonnage:

Number of Days on Board:

Distance logged:

Night hours/watch:

Details of voyage:

Crew/Position/Weather/Special duties/Incidents:

_____

_____

_____

_____

_____

Certifying Signature:
Captain or Owners Signature _____

Captain's Log ASA Documented Sailing Time

Dates   Leave: Arrive:

Times   Leave: Arrive:

Location   Origin:

                  Destination:

VesselName: LOA:

Type: Size: Tonnage:

Number of Days on Board:

Distance logged:

Night hours/watch:

Details of voyage:

            Crew/Position/Weather/Special duties/Incidents:

_____

_____

_____

_____

Certifying Signature:
Captain or Owners Signature   _____

Captain's Log ASA Documented Sailing Time

Dates   Leave: Arrive:

Times   Leave: Arrive:

Location   Origin:

                    Destination:

Vessel Name: LOA:

Type: Size: Tonnage:

Number of Days on Board:

Distance logged:

Night hours/watch:

Details of voyage:

Crew/Position/Weather/Special duties/Incidents:

_____

_____

_____

_____

Certifying Signature:
Captain or Owners Signature   _____

Captain's Log ASA Documented Sailing Time

Dates Leave: Arrive:

Times Leave: Arrive:

Location Origin:

Destination:

VesselName: LOA:

Type: Size: Tonnage:

Number of Days on Board:

Distance logged:

Night hours/watch:

Details of voyage:

Crew/Position/Weather/Special duties/Incidents:

_____

_____

_____

Certifying Signature:
Captain or Owners Signature _____

Captain's Log ASA Documented Sailing Time

Dates   Leave: Arrive:

Times   Leave: Arrive:

Location   Origin:

                 Destination:

VesselName: LOA:

Type: Size: Tonnage:

Number of Days on Board:

Distance logged:

Night hours/watch:

Details of voyage:

Crew/Position/Weather/Special duties/Incidents:

_____

_____

_____

_____

_____

Certifying Signature:
Captain or Owners Signature _____

Captain's Log ASA Documented Sailing Time

Dates   Leave: Arrive:

Times   Leave: Arrive:

Location   Origin:

                    Destination:

VesselName: LOA:

Type: Size: Tonnage:

Number of Days on Board:

Distance logged:

Night hours/watch:

Details of voyage:

                    Crew/Position/Weather/Special duties/Incidents:

_____

_____

_____

_____

Certifying Signature:
Captain or Owners Signature   _____

Captain's Log ASA Documented Sailing Time

Dates   Leave: Arrive:

Times   Leave: Arrive:

Location   Origin:

                   Destination:

VesselName: LOA:

Type: Size: Tonnage:

Number of Days on Board:

Distance logged:

Night hours/watch:

Details of voyage:

Crew/Position/Weather/Special duties/Incidents:

_____

_____

_____

_____

Certifying Signature:
Captain or Owners Signature   _____

Captain's Log ASA Documented Sailing Time

Dates   Leave: Arrive:

Times   Leave: Arrive:

Location   Origin:

                   Destination:

Vessel Name: LOA:

Type: Size: Tonnage:

Number of Days on Board:

Distance logged:

Night hours/watch:

Details of voyage:

Crew/Position/Weather/Special duties/Incidents:

_____

_____

_____

_____

Certifying Signature:
Captain or Owners Signature   _____

Captain's Log ASA Documented Sailing Time

Dates   Leave: Arrive:

Times   Leave: Arrive:

Location   Origin:

                        Destination:

Vessel Name: LOA:

Type: Size: Tonnage:

Number of Days on Board:

Distance logged:

Night hours/watch:

Details of voyage:

          Crew/Position/Weather/Special duties/Incidents:

_____

_____

_____

_____

Certifying Signature:
Captain or Owners Signature _____

Captain's Log ASA Documented Sailing Time

Dates   Leave: Arrive:

Times   Leave: Arrive:

Location   Origin:

                        Destination:

Vessel Name: LOA:

Type: Size: Tonnage:

Number of Days on Board:

Distance logged:

Night hours/watch:

Details of voyage:

                Crew/Position/Weather/Special duties/Incidents:

_____

_____

_____

_____

Certifying Signature:
Captain or Owners Signature   _____

Captain's Log ASA Documented Sailing Time

Dates　　Leave:　　　　　　　　Arrive:

Times　　Leave:　　　　　　　　Arrive:

Location　　Origin:

　　　　　　　Destination:

VesselName:　　　　　　　　LOA:

Type:　　　　　　　Size:　　　　　　Tonnage:

Number of Days on Board:

Distance logged:

Night hours/watch:

Details of voyage:

Crew/Position/Weather/Special duties/Incidents:

_____

_____

_____

_____

Certifying Signature:
Captain or Owners Signature _____

Captain's Log ASA Documented Sailing Time

Dates   Leave: Arrive:

Times   Leave: Arrive:

Location   Origin:

                    Destination:

VesselName: LOA:

Type: Size: Tonnage:

Number of Days on Board:

Distance logged:

Night hours/watch:

Details of voyage:

Crew/Position/Weather/Special duties/Incidents:

_____

_____

_____

_____

Certifying Signature:
Captain or Owners Signature _____

Captain's Log ASA Documented Sailing Time

Dates   Leave: Arrive:

Times   Leave: Arrive:

Location   Origin:

                   Destination:

VesselName: LOA:

Type: Size: Tonnage:

Number of Days on Board:

Distance logged:

Night hours/watch:

Details of voyage:

Crew/Position/Weather/Special duties/Incidents:

_____

_____

_____

_____

Certifying Signature:
Captain or Owners Signature _____

Captain's Log ASA Documented Sailing Time

Dates   Leave: Arrive:

Times   Leave: Arrive:

Location   Origin:

              Destination:

VesselName: LOA:

Type: Size: Tonnage:

Number of Days on Board:

Distance logged:

Night hours/watch:

Details of voyage:

          Crew/Position/Weather/Special duties/Incidents:

_____

_____

_____

_____

Certifying Signature:
Captain or Owners Signature _____

Captain's Log ASA Documented Sailing Time

Dates   Leave: Arrive:

Times   Leave: Arrive:

Location   Origin:

Destination:

Vessel Name: LOA:

Type: Size: Tonnage:

Number of Days on Board:

Distance logged:

Night hours/watch:

Details of voyage:

Crew/Position/Weather/Special duties/Incidents:

_____

_____

_____

_____

_____

Certifying Signature:
Captain or Owners Signature _____

Captain's Log ASA Documented Sailing Time

Dates   Leave: Arrive:

Times   Leave: Arrive:

Location   Origin:

                        Destination:

VesselName: LOA:

Type: Size: Tonnage:

Number of Days on Board:

Distance logged:

Night hours/watch:

Details of voyage:

                    Crew/Position/Weather/Special duties/Incidents:

_____

_____

_____

_____

Certifying Signature:
Captain or Owners Signature   _____

Captain's Log ASA Documented Sailing Time

Dates   Leave: Arrive:

Times   Leave: Arrive:

Location   Origin:

                      Destination:

Vessel Name: LOA:

Type: Size: Tonnage:

Number of Days on Board:

Distance logged:

Night hours/watch:

Details of voyage:

          Crew/Position/Weather/Special duties/Incidents:

_____

_____

_____

_____

Certifying Signature:

Captain or Owners Signature _____

Captain's Log ASA Documented Sailing Time

Dates   Leave: Arrive:

Times   Leave: Arrive:

Location   Origin:

Destination:

VesselName: LOA:

Type: Size: Tonnage:

Number of Days on Board:

Distance logged:

Night hours/watch:

Details of voyage:

Crew/Position/Weather/Special duties/Incidents:

_____

_____

_____

_____

Certifying Signature:
Captain or Owners Signature   _____

Captain's Log ASA Documented Sailing Time

Dates   Leave: Arrive:

Times   Leave: Arrive:

Location   Origin:

              Destination:

VesselName: LOA:

Type: Size: Tonnage:

Number of Days on Board:

Distance logged:

Night hours/watch:

Details of voyage:

Crew/Position/Weather/Special duties/Incidents:

_____

_____

_____

_____

_____

Certifying Signature:
Captain or Owners Signature _____

Captain's Log ASA Documented Sailing Time

Dates   Leave: Arrive:

Times   Leave: Arrive:

Location   Origin:

                   Destination:

VesselName: LOA:

Type: Size: Tonnage:

Number of Days on Board:

Distance logged:

Night hours/watch:

Details of voyage:

Crew/Position/Weather/Special duties/Incidents:

_____

_____

_____

_____

_____

Certifying Signature:
Captain or Owners Signature   _____

Captain's Log ASA Documented Sailing Time

Dates　　　Leave:　　　　　　　　Arrive:

Times　　　Leave:　　　　　　　　Arrive:

Location　　　Origin:

　　　　　　　Destination:

VesselName:　　　　　　　　　　LOA:

Type:　　　　　　　Size:　　　　　　Tonnage:

Number of Days on Board:

Distance logged:

Night hours/watch:

Details of voyage:

　　　　　Crew/Position/Weather/Special duties/Incidents:

_____

_____

_____

_____

Certifying Signature:
Captain or Owners Signature　_____

Captain's Log ASA Documented Sailing Time

Dates   Leave: Arrive:

Times   Leave: Arrive:

Location   Origin:

Destination:

VesselName: LOA:

Type: Size: Tonnage:

Number of Days on Board:

Distance logged:

Night hours/watch:

Details of voyage:

Crew/Position/Weather/Special duties/Incidents:

_____

_____

_____

_____

Certifying Signature:
Captain or Owners Signature _____

Captain's Log ASA Documented Sailing Time

Dates   Leave: _____   Arrive: _____

Times   Leave: _____   Arrive: _____

Location   Origin: _____

Destination: _____

VesselName: _____   LOA: _____

Type: _____   Size: _____   Tonnage: _____

Number of Days on Board: _____

Distance logged: _____

Night hours/watch: _____

Details of voyage: _____

Crew/Position/Weather/Special duties/Incidents:

_____

_____

_____

_____

Certifying Signature:
Captain or Owners Signature _____

Captain's Log ASA Documented Sailing Time

Dates   Leave: Arrive:

Times   Leave: Arrive:

Location   Origin:

               Destination:

VesselName: LOA:

Type: Size: Tonnage:

Number of Days on Board:

Distance logged:

Night hours/watch:

Details of voyage:

Crew/Position/Weather/Special duties/Incidents:

_____

_____

_____

_____

Certifying Signature:
Captain or Owners Signature   _____

Captain's Log ASA Documented Sailing Time

Dates   Leave: Arrive:

Times   Leave: Arrive:

Location   Origin:

                Destination:

VesselName: LOA:

Type: Size: Tonnage:

Number of Days on Board:

Distance logged:

Night hours/watch:

Details of voyage:

         Crew/Position/Weather/Special duties/Incidents:

_____

_____

_____

_____

_____

Certifying Signature:
Captain or Owners Signature   _____

Captain's Log ASA Documented Sailing Time

Dates   Leave: Arrive:

Times   Leave: Arrive:

Location   Origin:

                Destination:

VesselName: LOA:

Type: Size: Tonnage:

Number of Days on Board:

Distance logged:

Night hours/watch:

Details of voyage:

       Crew/Position/Weather/Special duties/Incidents:

_____

_____

_____

Certifying Signature:
Captain or Owners Signature _____

Captain's Log ASA Documented Sailing Time

Dates   Leave: Arrive:

Times   Leave: Arrive:

Location   Origin:

                   Destination:

VesselName: LOA:

Type: Size: Tonnage:

Number of Days on Board:

Distance logged:

Night hours/watch:

Details of voyage:

Crew/Position/Weather/Special duties/Incidents:

_____

_____

_____

_____

_____

Certifying Signature:
Captain or Owners Signature   _____

Captain's Log ASA Documented Sailing Time

Dates   Leave: Arrive:

Times   Leave: Arrive:

Location   Origin:

Destination:

VesselName: LOA:

Type: Size: Tonnage:

Number of Days on Board:

Distance logged:

Night hours/watch:

Details of voyage:

Crew/Position/Weather/Special duties/Incidents:

_____

_____

_____

_____

Certifying Signature:
Captain or Owners Signature _____

Captain's Log ASA Documented Sailing Time

Dates   Leave: Arrive:

Times   Leave: Arrive:

Location   Origin:

                   Destination:

VesselName: LOA:

Type: Size: Tonnage:

Number of Days on Board:

Distance logged:

Night hours/watch:

Details of voyage:

Crew/Position/Weather/Special duties/Incidents:

_____

_____

_____

_____

Certifying Signature:
Captain or Owners Signature _____

Captain's Log ASA Documented Sailing Time

Dates   Leave: Arrive:

Times   Leave: Arrive:

Location   Origin:

Destination:

VesselName: LOA:

Type: Size: Tonnage:

Number of Days on Board:

Distance logged:

Night hours/watch:

Details of voyage:

Crew/Position/Weather/Special duties/Incidents:

_____

_____

_____

_____

Certifying Signature:
Captain or Owners Signature   _____

Captain's Log ASA Documented Sailing Time

Dates   Leave: Arrive:

Times   Leave: Arrive:

Location   Origin:

                        Destination:

VesselName: LOA:

Type: Size: Tonnage:

Number of Days on Board:

Distance logged:

Night hours/watch:

Details of voyage:

Crew/Position/Weather/Special duties/Incidents:

_____

_____

_____

_____

Certifying Signature:
Captain or Owners Signature _____

Captain's Log ASA Documented Sailing Time

Dates   Leave: Arrive:

Times   Leave: Arrive:

Location   Origin:

                        Destination:

VesselName: LOA:

Type: Size: Tonnage:

Number of Days on Board:

Distance logged:

Night hours/watch:

Details of voyage:

Crew/Position/Weather/Special duties/Incidents:

_____

_____

_____

_____

Certifying Signature:
Captain or Owners Signature   _____

Captain's Log ASA Documented Sailing Time

Dates   Leave: Arrive:

Times   Leave: Arrive:

Location   Origin:

                 Destination:

VesselName: LOA:

Type: Size: Tonnage:

Number of Days on Board:

Distance logged:

Night hours/watch:

Details of voyage:

                 Crew/Position/Weather/Special duties/Incidents:

_____

_____

_____

_____

Certifying Signature:
Captain or Owners Signature _____

Captain's Log ASA Documented Sailing Time

Dates   Leave: Arrive:

Times   Leave: Arrive:

Location   Origin:

Destination:

VesselName: LOA:

Type: Size: Tonnage:

Number of Days on Board:

Distance logged:

Night hours/watch:

Details of voyage:

Crew/Position/Weather/Special duties/Incidents:

_____

_____

_____

_____

Certifying Signature:

Captain or Owners Signature _____

Captain's Log ASA Documented Sailing Time

Dates   Leave: Arrive:

Times   Leave: Arrive:

Location   Origin:

                Destination:

VesselName: LOA:

Type: Size: Tonnage:

Number of Days on Board:

Distance logged:

Night hours/watch:

Details of voyage:

           Crew/Position/Weather/Special duties/Incidents:

_____

_____

_____

_____

Certifying Signature:
Captain or Owners Signature   _____

Captain's Log ASA Documented Sailing Time

Dates   Leave: Arrive:

Times   Leave: Arrive:

Location   Origin:

                 Destination:

VesselName: LOA:

Type: Size: Tonnage:

Number of Days on Board:

Distance logged:

Night hours/watch:

Details of voyage:

Crew/Position/Weather/Special duties/Incidents:

_____

_____

_____

_____

Certifying Signature:
Captain or Owners Signature _____

Captain's Log ASA Documented Sailing Time

Dates   Leave: Arrive:

Times   Leave: Arrive:

Location   Origin:

                Destination:

VesselName: LOA:

Type: Size: Tonnage:

Number of Days on Board:

Distance logged:

Night hours/watch:

Details of voyage:

                Crew/Position/Weather/Special duties/Incidents:

_____

_____

_____

_____

_____

Certifying Signature:
Captain or Owners Signature _____

Captain's Log ASA Documented Sailing Time

Dates   Leave: Arrive:

Times   Leave: Arrive:

Location   Origin:

Destination:

VesselName: LOA:

Type: Size: Tonnage:

Number of Days on Board:

Distance logged:

Night hours/watch:

Details of voyage:

Crew/Position/Weather/Special duties/Incidents:

_____

_____

_____

_____

Certifying Signature:
Captain or Owners Signature   _____

Captain's Log ASA Documented Sailing Time

Dates   Leave: Arrive:

Times   Leave: Arrive:

Location   Origin:

                   Destination:

VesselName: LOA:

Type: Size: Tonnage:

Number of Days on Board:

Distance logged:

Night hours/watch:

Details of voyage:

          Crew/Position/Weather/Special duties/Incidents:

_____

_____

_____

_____

Certifying Signature:

Captain or Owners Signature   _____

Captain's Log ASA Documented Sailing Time

Dates   Leave: Arrive:

Times   Leave: Arrive:

Location   Origin:

                    Destination:

VesselName: LOA:

Type: Size: Tonnage:

Number of Days on Board:

Distance logged:

Night hours/watch:

Details of voyage:

Crew/Position/Weather/Special duties/Incidents:

_____

_____

_____

_____

Certifying Signature:
Captain or Owners Signature _____

Captain's Log ASA Documented Sailing Time

Dates   Leave: Arrive:

Times   Leave: Arrive:

Location   Origin:

             Destination:

VesselName: LOA:

Type: Size: Tonnage:

Number of Days on Board:

Distance logged:

Night hours/watch:

Details of voyage:

             Crew/Position/Weather/Special duties/Incidents:

_____

_____

_____

_____

_____

Certifying Signature:
Captain or Owners Signature   _____

Captain's Log ASA Documented Sailing Time

Dates   Leave: Arrive:

Times   Leave: Arrive:

Location   Origin:

                  Destination:

VesselName: LOA:

Type: Size: Tonnage:

Number of Days on Board:

Distance logged:

Night hours/watch:

Details of voyage:

        Crew/Position/Weather/Special duties/Incidents:

_____

_____

_____

_____

Certifying Signature:
Captain or Owners Signature   _____

Captain's Log ASA Documented Sailing Time

Dates Leave: Arrive:

Times Leave: Arrive:

Location Origin:

      Destination:

VesselName: LOA:

Type: Size: Tonnage:

Number of Days on Board:

Distance logged:

Night hours/watch:

Details of voyage:

Crew/Position/Weather/Special duties/Incidents:

_____

_____

_____

_____

_____

Certifying Signature:
Captain or Owners Signature _____

Captain's Log ASA Documented Sailing Time

Dates Leave: Arrive:

Times Leave: Arrive:

Location Origin:

Destination:

VesselName: LOA:

Type: Size: Tonnage:

Number of Days on Board:

Distance logged:

Night hours/watch:

Details of voyage:

Crew/Position/Weather/Special duties/Incidents:

_____

_____

_____

_____

_____

Certifying Signature:

Captain or Owners Signature _____

Captain's Log ASA Documented Sailing Time

Dates   Leave: Arrive:

Times   Leave: Arrive:

Location   Origin:

                    Destination:

Vessel Name: LOA:

Type: Size: Tonnage:

Number of Days on Board:

Distance logged:

Night hours/watch:

Details of voyage:

                    Crew/Position/Weather/Special duties/Incidents:

_____

_____

_____

_____

_____

Certifying Signature:
Captain or Owners Signature _____

Captain's Log ASA Documented Sailing Time

Dates   Leave: Arrive:

Times   Leave: Arrive:

Location   Origin:

                 Destination:

VesselName: LOA:

Type: Size: Tonnage:

Number of Days on Board:

Distance logged:

Night hours/watch:

Details of voyage:

Crew/Position/Weather/Special duties/Incidents:

_____

_____

_____

_____

Certifying Signature:
Captain or Owners Signature _____

Captain's Log ASA Documented Sailing Time

Dates   Leave: Arrive:

Times   Leave: Arrive:

Location   Origin:

                   Destination:

VesselName: LOA:

Type: Size: Tonnage:

Number of Days on Board:

Distance logged:

Night hours/watch:

Details of voyage:

Crew/Position/Weather/Special duties/Incidents:

_____

_____

_____

_____

_____

Certifying Signature:
Captain or Owners Signature _____

Captain's Log ASA Documented Sailing Time

Dates   Leave: Arrive:

Times   Leave: Arrive:

Location   Origin:

                   Destination:

VesselName: LOA:

Type: Size: Tonnage:

Number of Days on Board:

Distance logged:

Night hours/watch:

Details of voyage:

Crew/Position/Weather/Special duties/Incidents:

_____

_____

_____

_____

Certifying Signature:

Captain or Owners Signature   _____

Made in the USA
Middletown, DE
11 July 2022